SEASHORE DISCOVERIES

by

Wesley M. Farmer, Ph.D.

With 240 line drawings by the author

Front cover: Tidepoolers sharing sea life (inset). Background photo, Bird Rock, La Jolla, California at ebb tide. Photos by Wesley M. Farmer.

Back cover: Biography. Photo by Barbara L. Farmer.

Library of Congress Catalog Card Number: 84-91855

ISBN Number: 0-937772-01-1

First Edition: Dr. Wesley M. Farmer
P.O. Box 1323
Santee, CA 92071

Printed in the United States of America

DEDICATION

To my wife, Barbara
and children, Audrey and
Deanna, Deidre and Valerie

Octopus with a blue false eye below the real one. Photo by Wesley M. Farmer.

Navanax in a front view, note the dark eye spot in the field of white. Photo by Hans Bertsch.

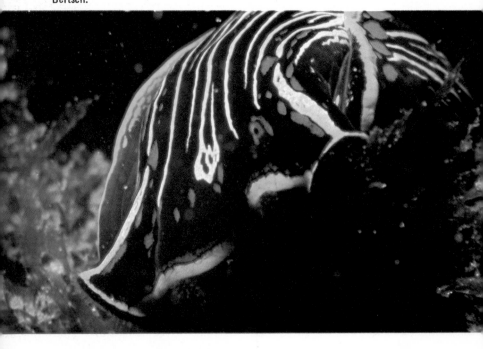

The nudibranch *Hopkinsia rosacea* shows two rhinophores at the right and six gills left of center. The animal is soft and flexible. Photo by Jeff Hamann.

Heart Urchin "walking" over the mudflat at low tide between bird tracks. Photo by Wesley M. Farmer.

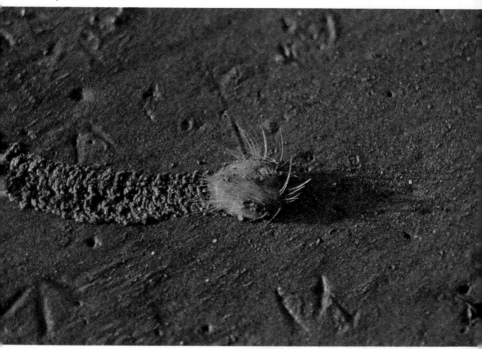

TIDEPOOLS CLEAR

Sky blue,

      green seas,

Sea gulls feeding.

      Snails burrowing.

Wet sand drenched.

Tides,

      Pushing sea weed,

Living creatures

      To be lost or reclaimed.

Sky blue,

      green seas,

Glimmering pools.

      Tidepools by moonlight,

Early morning sun,

      Twilight mist.

Thomas Parker Emery

PREFACE

It is intended that the scope of this work will interest persons in the more readily abundant or common sea life. Those with more time to search the tidepools may find the organisms that are more rare and elusive.

Some of this material appeared in One Hundred Common Marine Animals of San Diego published by the San Diego Natural History Museum where I was Curator of Exhibits. It is here updated and expanded to 240 drawings by the author. Some color photos, half-tone photos and drawings are presented to emphasize the features of the organisms.

Drawings were made with India black ink and crow quill pen. Some were drawn with Koh-I-Noor drawing pens. The color photos were exposed with a single lens reflex camera using extension bellows for close up work. Dr. Bertsch's picture of *Navanax* is an in situ underwater photograph taken with a Nikonos II and a 1:1 extension tube.

In the interest of conservation, those rock hoppers (people) who venture to the beach should be aware that the wildlife under foot are in their natural habitat. When looking under a rock please roll it back so that the animals and plants are not disturbed from their foothold. Picture taking is encouraged; specimens are best left in the habitat for which they evolved.

My thanks to those who have helped in one way or another in the production of this book. The hands on the cover are those of Deanna R. Farmer, Barbara L. Farmer, Deidre Speth and Jerry Jacobs. Appreciation is given to readers of the manuscript: Anna Stav, my wife Barbara, and Dr. Hans Bertsch. Special thanks to Jeff Hamann, Dave Mulliner and Don Wilkie for their review and opinion of the book prior to publication.

ALGAE / FLOWERING PLANT

The algae are an important part of our seashores. There are blue-green, green, red and brown algae. They range in size from microscopic to 300 foot long giant kelp. The algae provide shelter, camouflage, food, and foothold to live upon, and they garnish tidepools for special beauty and for us to wonder about as we look at them. They support a large industry that extracts special chemicals that are used in products in our every day lives.

A. SURF GRASS, *Phyllospadix sp.* A green alga with long thin bright green leaves that is attached to rock ledges at very low tide. It is a true flowering plant and is very abundant.

B. SEA LETTUCE, *Ulva sp.* A green alga that has broad bright breen blades. It is abundant and may be like fuzz on a rock or with blades an inch or two long, or even very large blades in bays.

C. DEAD MAN'S FINGERS, *Codium sp.* It is fairly common in the rocky inter-tidal area. Grows as clumps of dark matte green pencil-thick branches with six inch long flexible stems.

D. CORALLINE ALGAE, *Bossea sp.* A red alga, pink in color, with hard calcified heart shaped segments to its branching shoots. Grows to about three inches long and is abundant.

E. SEA GRAPES, *Botryocladia sp.* The red alga has vesicles appearing like a bunch of grapes. This alga is not readily seen along the rocky beach.

F. BATH TOWEL ALGAE, *Gigartina sp.* Broad blades of algae suggest the texture of terry cloth. Short bumps cover the blade. It is a red alga that is reasonably dark in color.

G. PUFFBALL ALGAE, *Colpomenia sp.* A light yellow-brown, brown alga that is thin and hollow, the inside filled with gas. The plants are irregularly round and live mostly in clusters.

H. FEATHER-BOA, *Egregia sp.* Very long broad blade with smaller fronds at the edges is seen. It is a brown alga and usually washes ashore. A close look may reveal shells that normally live on it.

I. ELK KELP, *Pelagophycus sp.* This kelp may usually be found on sandy beaches, washed ashore after being dislodged from its deep holdfast. A very long stipe with a gas bulb at the other end is what is so fascinating about this kelp. From this float arises two support branches and the very long broad fonds.

J. GIANT KELP, *Macrocystis sp.* Sandy beaches have had their share of this brown alga rolling in the surf or resting as a great tangle of stipes, fronds and hold-fast on the beach. This alga is of commercial interest. The plant growing in 100 feet of water grows as much as a foot a day.

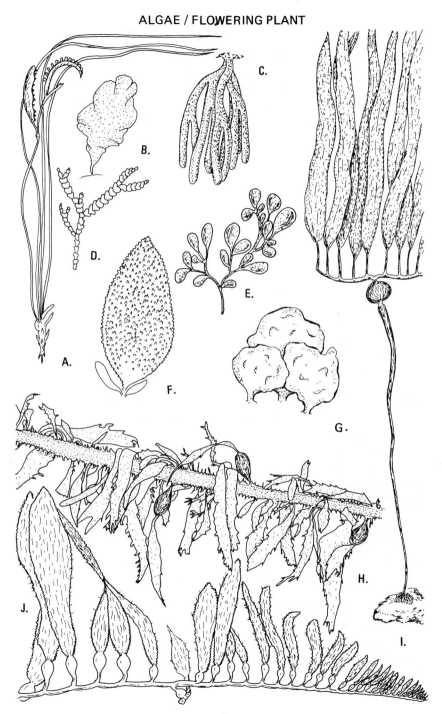

SPONGES - PORIFERA

The sponges are very primitive sedentary animals, which you might scarcely recognize as animals at all. Some live in fresh water, but most are marine. Water taken in through pores and circulated through canals carries food and oxygen to all parts of the animal. The skeleton of the sponge is of fibrous material (spongin) or of glassy or calcareous spicules. Bath sponges are the skeletons of certain tropical sponges—or were before the days of plastics. Our local sponges have no commercial value.

YELLOW SPONGE, *Aplysina fistularis* (Pallas, 1766). Yellow sponges can grow to about seven or eight inches in diameter. The animal is yellow, with an occasional green or lavender surface and has a sulphur-like odor. The mollusk *Tylodina fungina* obtains its yellow color by feeding on this sponge. RANGE: Mostly cosmopolitan. LOCAL DISTRIBUTION: On the underside of rocks or at their lower outer edge in the low tide zone of the rocky coast.

SEA ANEMONES - CNIDARIA (Coelenterata)

The coelenterates (or Cnidaria) include jellyfish, sea anemones, and corals. They are entirely aquatic, with most species being ocean dwellers. The body has a single opening, the mouth, surrounded by tentacles that capture the food. The Portuguese man-of-war and various jellyfish are known and feared for their painful stings but the other coelenterates also have tiny posion hypodermics (nematocysts). The stinging cells of the sea anemone cannot penetrate the thick skin of our fingers, but don't stick your tongue in one.

GIANT GREEN SEA ANEMONE, *Anthopleura xanthogrammica* (Brandt, 1835). The sea anemone in open or feeding position, with numerous radiating tentacles, is truly a flower of the sea. When disturbed or when exposed by low tide, it contracts into a flabby ball covered with small rocks and bits of sand. The giant green anemone may reach a diameter of ten inches, but small ones one or two inches across are more common. The color varies from a brilliant deep green through white, lavender, and pink, but never red or maroon. RANGE: From Sitka, Alaska, to Panama. LOCAL DISTRIBUTION: In the tidepools and high tide zone.

PROLIFERATING ANEMONE, *Epiactis prolifera* Verrill, 1869. This anemone generally has a ring of five or six young around its base, where they develop from small pits. It is green-lavender or brown. The crown of tentacles may reach two inches in diameter. RANGE: Alaska to Point Loma, California. LOCAL DISTRIBUTION: On brown algae or under rocks along the rocky coasts and at times in Mission Bay.

10

SPONGE

Yellow Sponge

SEA ANEMONIES

Giant Green Sea Anemone

Proliferating Anemone

COELENTERATES

SEA PEN, *Stylatula elongata* (Gabb, 1863). This colony of coelenterates live partially buried in the mud. The colony is held in place by a bulb or expansion at the distal end. They are white and are about one foot long. RANGE: Tomales Bay to San Diego. LOCAL DISTRIBUTION: In the mud of bays.

SEA PEN, *Ptilosarcus gurneyi* (Gray, 1860). This colony of coelenterates live in deep water partially buried in the mud. It is capable of expanding to more than twice its size or to a length of about l5 inches. When contracted, the colony is red but orange and white when expanded. The upper part of the colony is white with red edging. RANGE: Gulf of Alaska to southern California. LOCAL DISTRIBUTION: Deep water.

SEA PANSY, *Renilla koellikeri* Pfefier, 1886. Many polyps or animals live in a colonial community on a heart-shaped disk or rachis with a peduncle at one edge. The rachis is violet with yellow dots scattered over it. The colony can be deflated one and one-half inch or an inflated three inches in diameter. RANGE: Southern California into Baja California. LOCAL DISTRIBUTION: It is found in San Diego and Mission Bays.

GORGONIAN CORAL, *Muricea appressa* (Verrill, 1864). Most of these colonies are developed into tall plant-like structures. The axial skeleton is composed of calcareous spicules, of spongy horny material, or of both. Along this skeleton are the hundreds of polyps equipped with tentacles to capture passing food. The gorgonian coral or sea fan has been recorded to reach a height of about ten feet. The ones around San Diego are considerably smaller. Gorgonian corals have been taken at depths of 12,000 feet. The gorgonian coral drawn here is from a specimen about six inches tall. RANGE: Orange County, California, to Peru. LOCAL DISTRIBUTION: Mission Bay flood control channel jetty and deeper water off our coast.

BURROWING ANEMONE, *Pachycerianthus fimbriatus* McMurrich, 1910. The tube in which the burrowing anemone lives can be as long as six feet. When the tide is out, the animal can pull down into the tube to prevent drying. The anemone is only shown partly expanded here but when fully expanded the slender tentacles spread out making a circle up to five inches in diameter. The animal is brown with darker bandings on the tentacles. RANGE: California. LOCAL DISTRIBUTION: In bay mudflats and protected sandy bottoms.

COELENTERATES

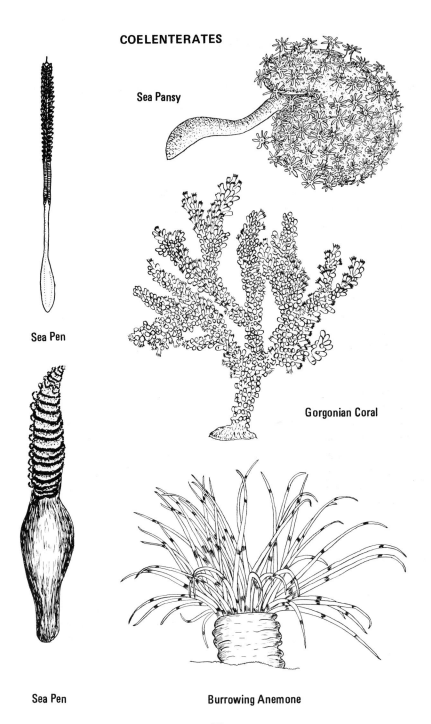

Sea Pansy

Sea Pen

Gorgonian Coral

Sea Pen

Burrowing Anemone

FLATWORMS - PLATYHELMINTHES

The flatworms comprise three classes whose best-known members are the parasitic tapeworms and flukes. Several free-living predaceous flatworms of the class Tubellaria may be seen by the visitor to the rocky sea shore. They are broad and flat, dark above and white beneath. One is the salt-and-pepper flatworm, which attains a length of about two inches. It is white with black specks. Another is light orange and still another an olive color. LOCAL DISTRIBUTION: Under rocks along the coast.

STRIPED FLATWORM, *Prostheceraeus bellostriatus* Hyman, 1953. The striped flatworm is exceptionally colored. It has black stripes on a white ground color, an orange line down the center of the body and an orange margin. The two tentacles in front are black. It attains a length of about an inch. RANGE: Monterey Bay to San Diego. LOCAL DISTRIBUTION: Rocky areas along the coast.

PAPILLATED FLATWORM, *Thysanozoon californicum* Hyman, 1953. Many papillae cover the back. This species has been used in neurophysiological research. It resembles a miniture shag carpet. It lives under rocks and is not abundant. RANGE: Southern California and northern Baja California. LOCAL DISTRIBUTION: Subtidal and under rocks.

MOSS ANIMALS - BRYOZOA

The moss animals (*Bryozoa*) are tiny animals forming sedentary colonies which often are mistaken for delicate seaweeds. A hand lens will reveal the numerous individuals, often no more than one-twenty-fifth of an inch across, each with a beak—like structure. The colonies of different kinds vary from feather-like to disk-shaped and may be several inches wide. Living moss animals vary in color from deep red-brown to white. Some appear as white disks on the fronds of kelp or as white patches on other algae. RANGE: World-wide. LOCAL DISTRIBUTION: On floats and docks in Mission Bay, on jetties and in rocky areas at very low tide. Kelp washed ashore usually has encrusting bryozoans on the kelp fronds.

Flatworms are highly colorful and beautiful creatures. They feed by a proboscus at the center of the underside of the very thin flat body. Some extend or contract their body shape when moving upon the underside of a rock. Some species swim by undulating their body in a wavy-like motion swimming through the water, perhaps to escape an irritation or simply move to another place.

14

FLATWORMS

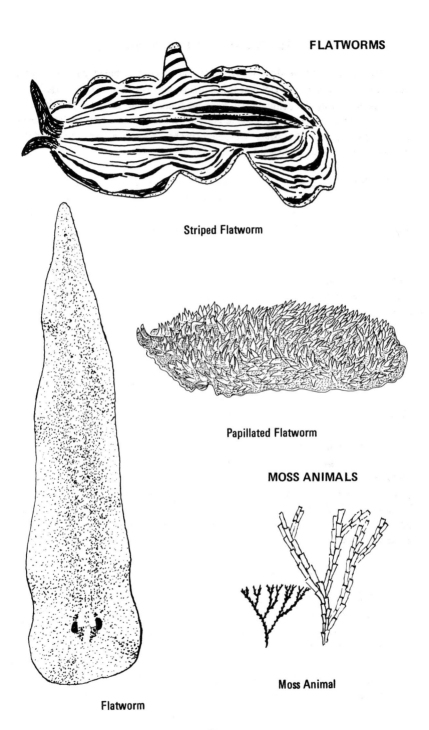

Striped Flatworm

Papillated Flatworm

MOSS ANIMALS

Moss Animal

Flatworm

15

SPIRORBID WORM, *Laeospira sp.* This spirorbid worm appears as a small white spot on just about everything. The calcareous tube is about one-sixteenth of an inch wide. The shell is white but is coiled to the right rather than to the left. RANGE: Various species along the Pacific coast of America. LOCAL DISTRIBUTION: Very common on rounded rocks and on kelp fronds that have washed ashore and occasionally on the backs of crabs and other solid surfaces.

PARCHMENT-TUBE WORM, *Chaetopterus variopedatus* (Renier, 1804). This segmented worm lives in a leathery, U-shaped tube of mucus. The worm has three projections near the center of the body used to fan water and food through its tube. The tube may be several feet long. It attains a length from 6 to 15 inches. It is yellow-white. RANGE: On this coast from Vancouver to San Diego, otherwise cosmopolitan in warm and temperate seas. LOCAL DISTRIBUTION: Mud flats of San Diego and Mission Bays.

SEA MOUSE, *Aphrodita armifera* Moore, 1910. The sea mouse is a large plump segmented worm covered with hair-like fibers giving it a soft appearance. The lateral fibers of this sea mouse are beautiful iridescent green, yellow, and blue. The back of the sea mouse is matted with very short fibers. There are strong strout spines at the upper edge of the fine fibers and on the lower edge. The segmentation of this annelid worm is clearly seen on the lower side. It is a dull olive drab with nearly black spines or setae and iridescent lateral fibers. It attains a length of about four inches. RANGE: Southern California well into Mexico. LOCAL DISTRIBUTION: Subtidal on muddy substrate.

POLYCHAETE, *Phragmatopoma californica* (Fewkes, 1889). The illustration dipects a few of the openings of their sand cemented tubes. The colony may cover several rocks. An operculum is used to close the opening to the tube or when open numerous tentacles are at work collecting detritus or sand grains to cement onto the numerous tubes. RANGE: Central California to Punta Baja, Baja California Norte. LOCAL DISTRIBUTION: From the lot tide area into subtidal regions on rocks.

RICH BROWN PEANUT WORM, *Themiste pyroides* (Chamberlin, 1919). When disturbed, the peanut worm is usually contracted into a peanut shape. If placed in a bottle of sea water for a while, it will extend its gill-tipped mouth, which is on the end of a long stalk. *Themiste pyroides* lives under rocks in the sandy substate, while *Themiste zostericola* (Chamberlin, 1919), a similar species, lives in the roots of surf grass. Both worms attain average lengths of about four inches. They appear smooth rich purple brown. RANGE: Vancouver Island, British Columbia, to Bahía De San Quintin, Baja California Norte. LOCAL DISTRIBUTION: Along the rocky coast at the low tide level.

SEGMENTED WORMS

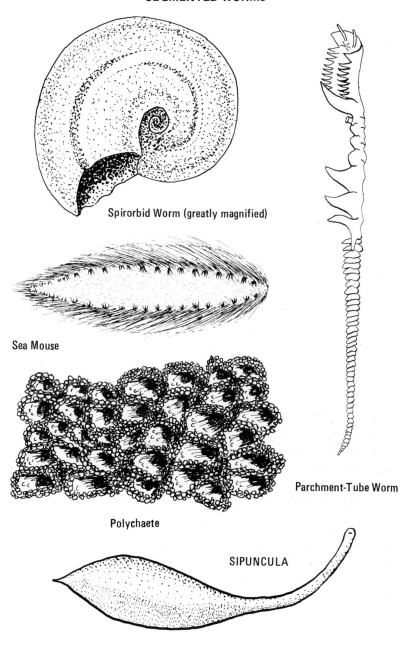

Spirorbid Worm (greatly magnified)

Sea Mouse

Polychaete

Parchment-Tube Worm

SIPUNCULA

Rich Brown Peanut Worm

17

ARTHROPODS

The arthropods make up the largest phylum of animals, and include the insects, spiders, centipedes and some others, found mostly on land, and the crustaceans which are a major marine group. The arthropod wears its skeleton outside like a suit of armor, with joints where it can bend. The name "arthropod" refers to the jointed legs. To grow after the skeleton has hardened, it must shed the skeleton and form a new one. The crustaceans include crabs, lobsters, shrimp, sand fleas, barnacles, and many others.

Barnacles at first glance, you might never suspect that barnacles are related to sand fleas, pill bugs, and crabs, for they grow attached to rocks and whales and things, and they have a protective outer covering. But inside this shell, the body and legs are jointed. The swimming larva looks more like a normal crustacean, but then it settles down on its back, develops a shell, and kicks its feet in the water to catch food. Some barnacles have volcano-shaped shells, attached directly to the rock or whatever, but the goose barnacles have a flexible stalk. The barnacles comprise the subclass Cirripedia.

LEAF BARNACLE, *Pollicipes polymerus* Sowerby, 1833. The leaf barnacle has a flexible stalk, and the upper end is encased in a series of valves through which food-capturing feet protrude. It attains a length of about three inches. RANGE: British Columbia to central Baja California. LOCAL DISTRIBUTION: Rocky headlands and pier pilings in the upper tide range, often with the California mussel.

GREAT BARNACLE, *Megabalanus californicus* (Pilsbry, 1916). This barnacle is about two and one-fourth inches in diameter. It has red and white up and down bars. RANGE: Humboldt Bay California, to Guaymas, Mexico. LOCAL DISTRIBUTION:

THATCHED BARNACLE, *Tetraclita rubescens* (Darwin, 1854). The thatched barnacle is sometimes solitary, but usually lives in clusters. The sides of the scutum (shell) give the appearance of being thatched; hence its name. It is up to one and one-fourth inches wide. It is light pink or red, but at times it appears green because of green algae which grow on it. RANGE: Farallon Island, California, to Cabo San Lucas, Baja California Sur. LOCAL DISTRIBUTION: Open rocky coasts.

ACORN BARNACLE, *Balanus glandula* Darwin, 1854. The acorn barnacle is dingy white with heavily ribbed plates. It reaches a diameter of nearly three-fourths of an inch. It is white to gray and has a variable shape. It is very common. RANGE: Aleutian Islands, Alaska, to Bahía San Quintin, Baja California Norte. LOCAL DISTRIBUTION: Common on rocky coasts and especially on rocks in bays, in the upper tidal area.

BARNACLES

SMALL ACORN BARNACLE, *Chthamalus fissus* Darwin, 1854. The small acorn barnacle is found in close association with the acorn barnacle, from which it is readily distinguished by its neat smooth surface, its lesser width (about one-fourth inch), and its darker color (dark tan). RANGE: San Francisco to Baja California. LOCAL DISTRIBUTION: Common in bays in the upper tidal zone and along the rocky coast.

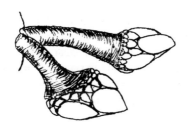

Leaf Barnacle

Great Barnacle

Thatched Barnacle

Acorn Barnacle   Small Acorn Barnacle

BARNACLES

RABBIT-EARED BARNACLE, *Conchoderma auritum* (Linnaeus, 1758). The rabbit-eared or stalked barnacle can be found under the chin of some whales; at times the hump-back whale has hundreds of them. This barnacle seems to do best on a firm support similar to what other barnacles provide. It attains a length of about eight inches. It is light colored with darker blotches and stripes. Ten or more barnacles may be attached to a single barnacle. RANGE: Cosmopolitan. LOCAL DISTRIBUTION: On barnacles on whales off our coast.

GOOSENECK BARNACLE, *Lepas fascicularis* Ellis & Solander, 1786. Clusters of these barnacles may be floating at the surface of the ocean by means of a bubble float. This barnacle has thin paper-like plates. It is whitish. The gooseneck barnacle attains a length of one-half inch. RANGE: Cosmopolitan. LOCAL DISTRIBUTION: Occasionally washes ashore after a storm, otherwise pelagic and not particularly uncommon.

WHALE BARNACLE, *Coronula diadema* (Linnaeus, 1767). This barnacle lives attached to whales and slightly embedded in the skin. This barnacle has a nearly round base with a diameter of two inches, slightly flattened with a height of about three-fourths of an inch. The barnacle is white. RANGE: Cosmopolitan. LOCAL DISTRIBUTION: It is common on whales.

ISOPODS

SAND PILL BUG, *Tylos sp.* This animal is similar to the garden pill bugs and will curl up into a ball (like a pill) when handled. It is about one and one-fourth inch long and is tan or light gray. Pill bugs belong to the group of crustaceans known as isopods. RANGE: Southern California. LOCAL DISTRIBUTION: Located by its mole-like holes on sandy beaches.

ROCK LOUSE, *Ligia occidentalis* Dana, 1853. This evasive animal is often seen in daylight moving about the rocks near the high tide line or in the spray zone. If submerged for a long time it will drown. It is about one and one-fourth inches long and is olive green or dark gray. RANGE: Sacramento River to the Gulf of California and central America. LOCAL DISTRIBUTION: On rocks in the spray zone and under drying kelp washed ashore near the rocks.

Panoramic vista views can be experienced at Cabrillo National Monument at the tip of Point Loma. There are tidepools for the nature lovers with parking near the site. Collecting is not permitted.

BARNACLES

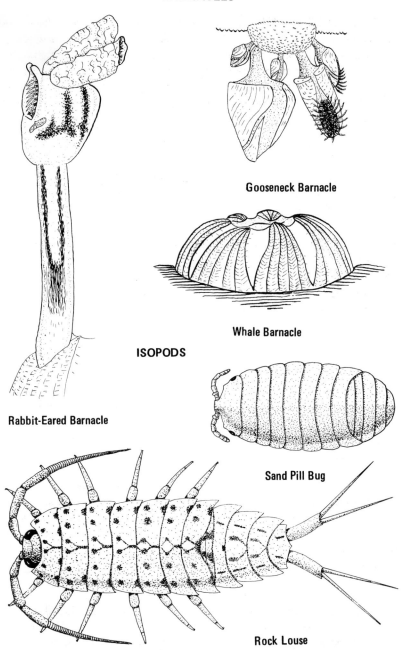

Gooseneck Barnacle

Whale Barnacle

Rabbit-Eared Barnacle

ISOPODS

Sand Pill Bug

Rock Louse

21

ISOPOD

ISOPOD, *Idotea spp.* Some related intertidal species cling to thin pieces of algae with the sharp tips of their legs. The species are usually colored like the green, brown or yellow-ochre colored algae or surfgrass they cling to. The tip of the last segment (tail) is one way to distinguish the different species because of the different shapes. They are dorso-venterally flattened. This species attains a length of three-fourths of an inch and is brown colored. RANGE: Humboldt county to southern California. LOCAL DISTRIBUTION: About rocks and algae.

ZOOPLANKTER

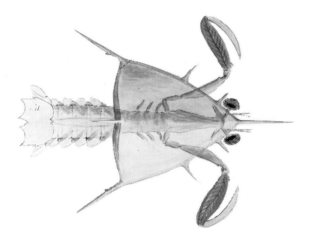

Microscopic zooplankter

The four different animals illustrated here in the two half-tones are zooplankters from the open ocean, a long way from the bottom or a rock. They must molt or shed their exoskeleton. While this exoskeleton is still soft, it expands a bit to a new larger size to harden for support and protection from predators. The two dark spots at the anterior end of the larval forms are compound eyes. The surface of the compound eyes are covered by many facets, one facet for each seeing component of the compound eyes.

ZOOPLANKTON

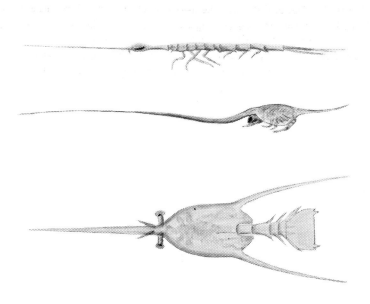

Microscopic transparent arthropod larval stage of a zooplankter or simply a baby crab as clear as glass is drawn here larger than life.

ISOPOD

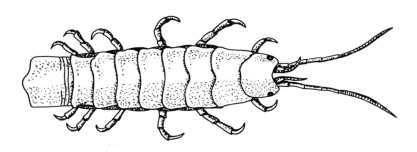

Isopod

AMPHIPOD

SKELETON SHRIMP or CAPRELLID, *Caprella californica* Stimpson, 1857. Caprellids are stick-like animals (amphipods) difficult to see because they blend so well with the tunicates, hydroids or algae to which they cling. They reach more than an inch long and are brownish. The female has a brood pouch to carry her eggs and larvae. It possesses a spine on the head. It grasps food with claws like a praying mantis. This shrimp stands upright and can swim by flexing its body. RANGE: Central and southern California. LOCAL DISTRIBUTION: Found commonly about the floats in bays.

AMPHIPOD or BEACH HOPPER, *Megalorchestia californiana* (Brandt, 1851). This crustacean is laterally flattened and one of some 150 species found in Southern California. This particular one is white. The base of the antennae is orange the back a light gray color and legs generally white. It attains a length of an inch. RANGE: Vancouver Island (British Columbia) to Laguna Beach, southern California. LOCAL DISTRIBUTION: Under kelp washed ashore. Other species are more common in this area.

SHRIMP

SPOTTED BAY SHRIMP, *Crangon nigromaculata* Lockington, 1877. The spotted bay shrimp has a prominent spot on each side of the sixth abdominal segment or the first one in from the tail. This spot has a bluish center with a black ring around it, then a yellow ring. It lives in deeper water and occurs occasionally in the shrimpers catch and is sold on the market as a food item or for bait. It should not be mistaken for the black-tailed shrimp which is more commonly sold in markets. The spotted bay shrimp attains a length of about one and one-half inch. RANGE: California and Mexico. LOCAL DISTRIBUTION: Subtidal.

Plankton are in two forms; phytoplankton and zooplankton, or simply very young plant and animal forms that drift in the ocean. Some always live there, like one-celled plants called diatoms or very small crustaceans called copepods. Young newly hatched crabs, lobsters, barnacles, mollusks and other forms drift for a spell before settling down on a rock, a piling, or the skin of a whale or the like to take up the process of feeding and growing up.

24

AMPHIPOD

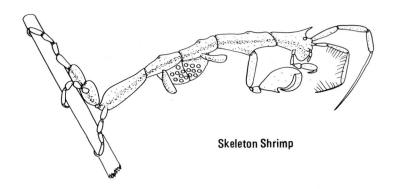

Skeleton Shrimp

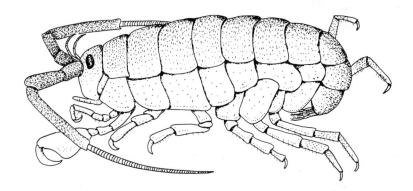

Beach Hopper or Sand Flea

SHRIMP

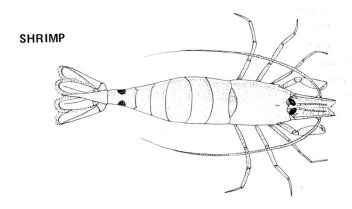

Spotted Bay Shrimp

25

SHRIMP

RED ROCK SHRIMP, *Lysmata californica* (Stimpson, 1866). As many as a dozen red rock shrimp can be found under a rock at the low tide level. They are also found in association with moray eels with which it may act as a cleaner. They move about quickly and are difficult to capture. The red rock shrimp is up to two and one-half inches long with even longer antennae. The body is transparent with numerous red stripes. RANGE: Santa Barbara, California, to Bahía Sebastian Vizcaino, Baja California. LOCAL DISTRIBUTION: Under rocks at the low tide level along the coast.

BROKEN-BACK SHRIMP, *Spirontocaris picta* (Stimpson, 1871). Though it is common, the broken-back shrimp is sometimes difficult to see because its color blends well with its tide pool background. It is up to an inch long. There are several similar shrimps, distinguished by head shape. RANGE: Southern California and also found in Baja California Norte. LOCAL DISTRIBUTION: In the tide pools of the rocky coast.

SNAPPING SHRIMP, *Alpheus clamator* Lockington, 1877. At times during a very low tide, one can hear the snapping sound caused by the elusive pistol shrimp. One claw is greatly enlarged and modified to produce this sound. If handled roughly, the claw will fall off, but later the animal will grow a new one. The snapping shrimp attains a length of about two inches and is mottled tan and green. RANGE: San Francisco, California, to Bahía San Bartolome, Baja California. LOCAL DISTRIBUTION: Generally found in the roots of surf grass at very low tide.

LONG-FINGERED SHRIMP, *Betaeus longidactylus* Lockington, 1877. The sexes of the long-fingered shrimp can be distinguished by their claws. The male, pictured here, has two extraordinarily long claws, generally half as long as the body. The female is small-clawed. The long-fingered shrimp is about two and one-half inches long. It varies from blue and blue-green to olive brown. RANGE: Monterey Bay to the Gulf of California. LOCAL DISTRIBUTION: Under rocks at low tide level and with the blue mud shrimp in bays.

SHRIMP, *Pandalus platyceros* Brandt, 1851. The rostrum of this shrimp is very long (greater than two inches) and slightly curved upward. The shrimp is spotted with red on a lighter ground color. There are dark bands on the legs and antennae. This shrimp attains a length of eight inches from the tip of the rostrum to the tip of the tail. The antennae are about seven inches long. RANGE: Bering Strait south to southern California and from Japan to Korea. LOCAL DISTRIBUTION: Deep water (to 487 meters depths) off San Diego.

The San Diego Zoo in Balboa Park displays live seals, elephant seals and other species of life found about the sea.

SHRIMP

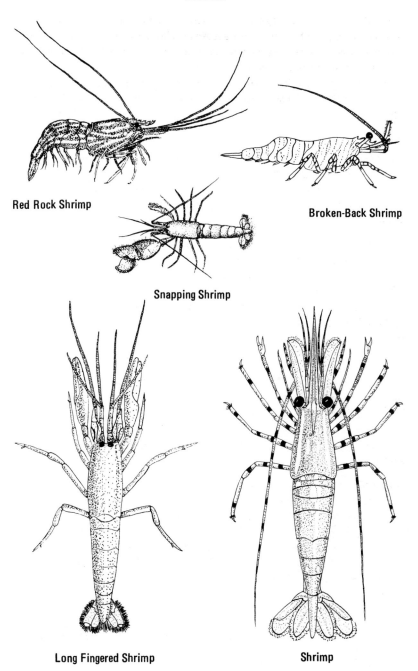

Red Rock Shrimp

Broken-Back Shrimp

Snapping Shrimp

Long Fingered Shrimp

Shrimp

27

BLUE SHRIMP, *Upogebia pugettensis* (Dana, 1852). This animal can be found inhabiting muddy beaches and occasionally in deeper water where they live in burrows. When alive, they have a muddy color. They attain a length of about two and one-half inches. RANGE: Alaska to lower California. LOCAL DISTRIBUTION: Muddy beaches of bays.

BEACH GHOST SHRIMP, *Callianassa affinis* Holmes, 1900. This shrimp lives in a commensal relationship in a tunnel in the sand with a pair of blind gobies. It is fairly common. This shrimp may be two and one-half inches long. It is dull white or cream colored. One claw is greatly enlarged. RANGE: Santa Barbara County to Bahía San Quintin, Baja California. LOCAL DISTRIBUTION: Under rocks of the protected rocky coast and in burrows in the sand substrate.

CALIFORNIA SPINY LOBSTER, *Panulirus interruptus* (Randall, 1840 Fide Sherborn). The California spiny lobster is occasionally seen in the tide pools at very low tide, particularly in the summer. It is red-brown and up to two feet long. RANGE: Point Conception, California, into Mexico. LOCAL DISTRIBUTION: On rocky shores near and below the low tide line.

Feeding the sea birds at Casa Beach, La Jolla.

SHRIMP / LOBSTER

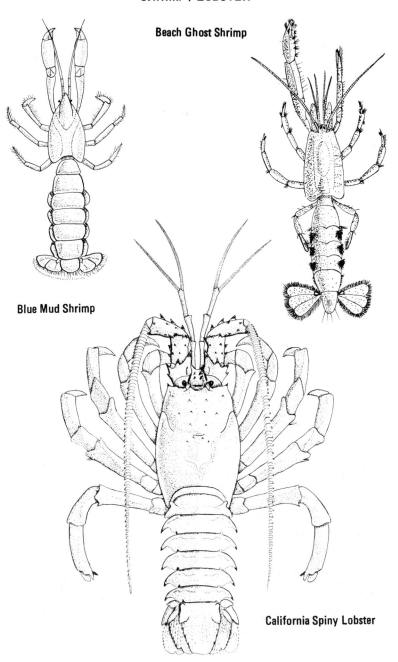

Beach Ghost Shrimp

Blue Mud Shrimp

California Spiny Lobster

COPEPOD

PARASITIC COPEPOD, *Pennella sp.* This unusually shaped ectoparasitic copepod attains a length of about ten inches. It is of a dark color. RANGE: Wherever its host might be found in the Atlantic or Pacific. LOCAL DISTRIBUTION: On flying fish, marlin, and whales, possibly other large creaters.

MANTIS SHRIMP

MANTIS SHRIMP, *Hemisquilla ensigera* (Owen, 1932). This shrimp is one of the most colorful, having an azure blue and orange body. The walking legs are blue, and the tail is blue and golden. It lives in a burrow that is up to four feet deep. It attains a length of a foot. RANGE: Point Conception south to Peru and Chile. LOCAL DISTRIBUTION: In muddy bottoms off our coast.

POLISHED SQUILLA, *Schmittius politus* (Bigelow, 1891). The claws of the polished squilla are large and flattened and armed with long spines. These claws fold under the thorax and are not seen in the drawing. The polished squilla attains a length of about three and one-half inches. RANGE: Monterey Bay, California, to Punta Abreojos, Baja California Sur. LOCAL DISTRIBUTION: Deep water off San Diego.

PYCNOGONID

SEA SPIDER, *Anoplodactylus erectus* Cole, 1904. Sea spiders are also known as pycnogonids. They are difficult to see because of their small size and color which blends so well with the background. The small abdomen in this species is erect. Sea spiders have the tendency to cling to objects, and if several were placed in a dish of sea water, they would eventually be clinging to each other. This animal attains a diameter of one-half inch. RANGE: Southern California. LOCAL DISTRIBUTION: Among seaweeds, hydroids and bryozoans in bays and along the coast.

COMMENSALISM involves two different species, such as the scale worm living about the tube feet of a seastar or the blind goby with the ghost shrimp, both living together but one benefits without harm to the other. In SYMBIOSIS both species need each other to survive, like the green algae inside the tissues of the coelenterate, producing oxygen and in turn the coelenterate produces carbon dioxide.

COPEPOD

skin section of vertebrate

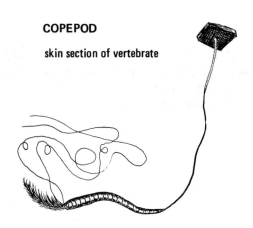

Parasitic Copepod

MANTIS SHRIMP

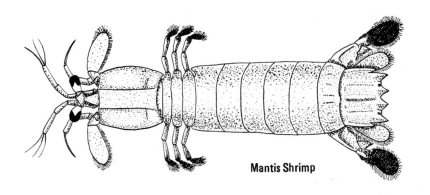

Mantis Shrimp

SEA SPIDER

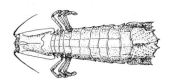

Polished Squilla

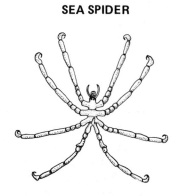

Sea Spider

CRABS

HERMIT CRAB, *Pagurus spp.* When you see a small shell moving at more than a snail's pace, very likely the snail doesn't live there any more. The hermit crab sets up housekeeping in an abandoned snail shell, and on outgrowing it, moves to another. The crab generally retracts into the shell when disturbed but will soon reappear if held still. Living in the snail shell near the opening along with the hermit crab, the white slipper shell (*Crepidula nummaria* Gould, 1846) can often be found. RANGE: Cosmopolitan. LOCAL DISTRIBUTION: On rocky beaches near the high tide line and on floats in bays. They tend to aggregate.

PORCELAIN CRAB, *Petrolisthes spp.* The porcelain crabs are extremely flattened and rounded with large, smooth, flat claws, which on occasion are quickly shed. They are olive green and usually under half an inch long. The antennae are on the outer side of the eyes and are extremely long. The porcelain crab, *P. cinctipes* (Randall, 1839), is common on the outer coast; another (*P. eriomerus* Stimpson, 1871), very similar in appearance, occurs in bays. RANGE: Pacific coast of America, and elsewhere. LOCAL DISTRIBUTION: Under rocks and in mussel beds and in Mission Bay on floats and pilings. When exposed, they scurry to hide.

THICK-CLAWED PORCELAIN CRAB, *Pachycheles rudis* Stimpson, 1859. The thick-clawed porcelain crab has large tuberculate chelipeds or claws, one being larger than the other. This crab attains a carapace width of about three-fourth of an inch. It is light brown. RANGE: British Columbia to lower California. LOCAL DISTRIBUTION: At low tide about rocks and in holes in the rocks along the coast.

TUNA or PELAGIC RED CRAB, *Pleuroncodes planipes* Stimpson 1860. The pelagic red crab has the habit of occasionally being stranded on the beach. Thousands will be washed ashore where they turn the beach red and pile up several inches deep. In 1960 great numbers appeared at Monterey Bay and in 1983 everywhere off San Diego. Their occurrence on the beach is far more common in the Gulf of California. This crab is closely related to the hermit crabs and sand crabs in that they have their antennae originating external to the eyes. This crab attains a length of 70 mm and is bright red. RANGE: Warm waters south of Monterey into the Gulf of California. DISTRIBUTION: Off shore usually found at night with the aid of a light where they come to the surface, though usually in deeper water. Fishermen may find them in the stomachs of rockfish.

The San Diego Natural History Museum in Balboa Park displays many species of marine fish, sea shells, shore birds and marine mammals and marine habitats.

32

CRABS

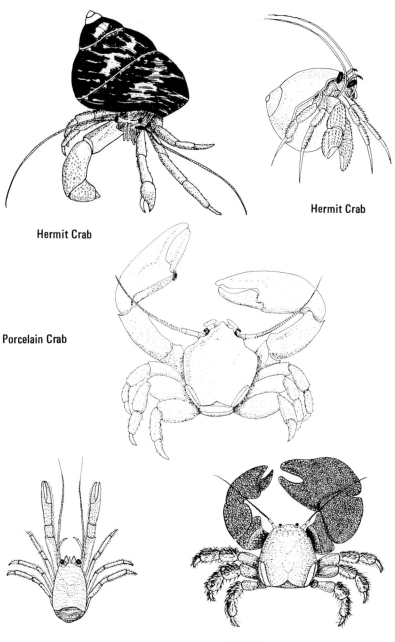

Hermit Crab

Hermit Crab

Porcelain Crab

Tuna or Pelagic Red Crab

Thick-Clawed Porcelain Crab

33

CRABS

HAIRY CANCER CRAB, *Cancer jordani* Rathbun, 1900. This cancer crab is particularly hairy. It is small, attaining a carapace width of one and one-fourth inches. The cancer crabs are good to eat and can also be found in fish markets. RANGE: Coos Bay, Oregon, to Cabo Thurloe, Baja California Sur. LOCAL DISTRIBUTION: Rocky tidepool areas along the coast.

GRACEFUL CANCER CRAB, *Cancer gracilis* Dana, 1852. This crab has a somewhat smooth carapace. The walking legs are slender and end in a sharp point. It is tan and dotted with red spots. It attains a carapace diameter of about two and one-half inches. RANGE: Aleutian Islands, to Bahía Magdalena, Baja California Sur. LOCAL DISTRIBUTION: Deeper water off the coast.

SHEEP CRAB, *Loxorhynchus grandis* Stimpson, 1857. The sheep crab lives below the low tide line. Although not particularly rare, they are seldom seen except by divers. One may be washed ashore after a severe storm. The walking legs are larger in front getting progressively smaller behind. The carapace or back measures,as much as eight inches long and six inches wide. The front legs measure more than ten inches long. RANGE: Marin County into Baja California. Oligocene fossils from Washington; Pliocene from central California; Pleistocene from Los Angeles County. LOCAL DISTRIBUTION: Sandy bottoms beyond the low tide line off our coast.

KELP CRAB or SHIELD-BACKED KELP CRAB, *Pugettia producta* (Randall, 1839). The kelp crab is easily distinguished by the straight, parallel sides of the carapace (back), each side bearing two large spines. The prominent rostrum (front) is deeply split. Small specimens under an inch are often found in algae. The carapace is smooth and up to three inches wide. The color varies with age small individuals are olive-brown above and spotted with white below; adults are brilliant red above and red with white spots below. RANGE: Alaska to Punta Asuncion, Baja California Sur. LOCAL DISTRIBUTION: Common on algae and surf grass in rocky areas.

SOUTHERN KELP CRAB, *Taliepus nuttallii* (Randall, 1839). The southern kelp crab lacks the prominent spines that the kelp crab has on the carapace. It is up to four inches across the carapace. It is dark red-brown. RANGE: Point Conception, California, to Bahía Magdalena, Baja California Sur. Pleistocene fossils have been found in Los Angeles County. LOCAL DISTRIBUTION: In surf grass and brown algae at the low tide line.

San Diego's Sea World displays some forms of offshore sea life to be viewed at close range. Other species from more distant places are on display also.

CRABS

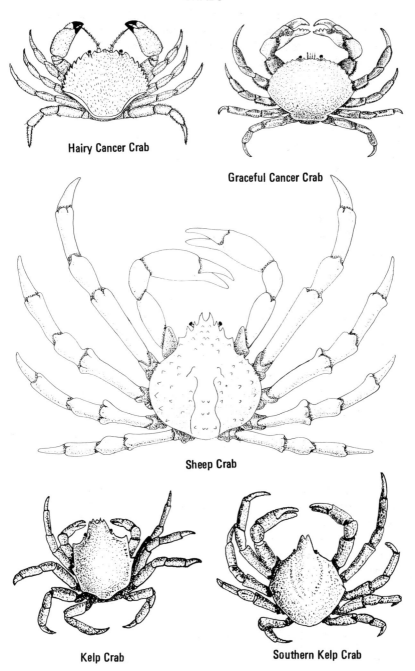

Hairy Cancer Crab

Graceful Cancer Crab

Sheep Crab

Kelp Crab

Southern Kelp Crab

CRABS

RED or LARGE PEBBLE CRAB, *Cycloxanthops novemdentatus* (Lockington, 1877). The claws and the front part of the carapace of the rad crab are covered with fine granules. The carapace is wider than long, is slightly flattened, and lacks the large triangular points typical of the *Cancer* crabs. A large individual may be two and one-half inches long and four inches wide. The red crab is brilliantly colored, varying from a bright red to a deep purple. RANGE: Monterey, California, to Punta Abreojos, Baja California Sur. LOCAL DISTRIBUTION: Under rocks, half covered with sand.

COMMON ROCK CRAB, *Cancer antennarius* Stimpson, 1856. The common rock crab is much wider than long; it reaches a length of four inches and a width of seven inches. Distinguishing characteristics are the black-tipped claws and the red spotting on its under surface; otherwise it is red-brown. The front edges of the carapace have prominent triangular projections. RANGE: Coos Bay Oregon to Islas de Todos Santos, Baja California. LOCAL DISTRIBUTION: Found about sand and rocks.

MASKING or MOSS CRAB, *Loxorhynchus crispatus* Stimpson, 1857. The masking crab is somewhat triangular, with a widely split rostrum (front) which points slightly downward. It reaches a length of four and one-half inches. The related sheep crab (*L. grandis*), less often seen, may be distinguished by its upturned rostrum and larger size. The masking crab's inflated carapace (back) and the legs bear short stiff hairs, to which it attaches small bits of seaweed, sponges, bryozoans, or whatever is available. This walking garden loses all resemblance to a crab. RANGE: Humboldt County, California, to Isla Natividad, Baja California Sur. LOCAL DISTRIBUTION: Found occasionally under ledges overgrown with algae.

LINED or STRIPED SHORE CRAB, *Pachygrapsus crassipes* Randall, 1839. The lined shore crab is most often seen along our coast. It feeds on both plant and animal material and hides under rocks when approached. It is generally deep red or green and attains a width of about two inches. RANGE: From Oregon south into the Gulf of California. LOCAL DISTRIBUTION: In all rocky areas of open coasts and bays and occasionally on floats and pilings.

YELLOW SHORE CRAB, *Hemigrapsus oregonensis* (Dana, 1851). Hairy legs are a distinctive characteristic of the yellow shore crab. This crab attains a width across the carapace of one inch. It is green-gray or yellow. RANGE: Alaska to Bahía de Todos Santos in Baja California Norte. LOCAL DISTRIBUTION: Under rocks and eel grass on the mud flats of San Diego and Mission bays.

Scripps Institute of Oceanography has a museum and aquarium of local and regional sea life with labels explaining them.

CRABS

Large Pebble Crab

Common Rock Crab

Masking Crab

Yellow Shore Crab

Lined Shore Crab

CRABS

ELBOW CRAB, *Heterocrypta occidentalis* (Dana, 1854). The triangular carapace and long chelipeds or claws give the elbow crab a distinctive look. It has light mottlings and is pinkish. The elbow crab attains a carapace of one and one-fourth inches with a cheliped length of two and three-fourth inches. RANGE: Monterey to Baja California. LOCAL DISTRIBUTION: Deep water off San Diego and sand flats.

PURPLE CRAB, *Randallia ornata* (Randall, 1839). The carapace of this animal is almost round, giving it a characteristic appearance. It is mottled with purple, flat orange or brown. The length and width of the purple crab is about two inches. RANGE: California southward. LOCAL DISTRIBUTION: In deeper water off our coast and on sand flats.

SWIMMING CRAB, *Portunus xantusii xantusii* (Stimpson, 1860). The last two segments of the last pair of legs are flattened into paddles for swimming sideways. There are very sharp spines on the sides of the carapace making this animal difficult to pick up. The crab is capable of burrowing into the sand until hidden. The swimming crab attains a carapace diameter of about two and one-half inches. RANGE: Santa Barbara to Topolobampo, Mexico. Pleistocene fossils have come from San Diego. LOCAL DISTRIBUTION: In eelgrass beds in Mission Bay, or on subtidal sand flats.

PEA CRAB or MUSSEL CRAB, *Fabia subquadrata* Dana, 185l. The palm of the claws have two rows of fine hairs. There are four grooves on the back. In this specimen the abdomen nearly covers the front of the crab. This pea crab is whitish with orange spots. It attains a width of one-half inch. The female lives inside other animals, the male does also but not as frequently. RANGE: Alaska to La Jolla. LOCAL DISTRIBUTION: In mussels and clams along the coast.

FIDDLER CRAB, *Uca crenulata crenulata* (Lockington, 1877). The female fiddler crab has two small claws of equal size. The male however has a small claw and one very large claw. Fiddler crabs live in the burrows just above the tide line. This crab is not particularly uncommon, but it requires a little effort in order to find them. It attains a carapace diameter of about three-fourth inch. The claw in the male is as much as one and one-fourth inches long. RANGE: Los Angeles County to Lower California. LOCAL DISTRIBUTION: Sloughs and bays of the San Diego area. Former large colonies in Mission Bay are apparently facing extinction.

Jacques Costeau was primarily responsible for the invention of the Aqua Lung. A diver can spend some time underwater viewing or photographing some of the spectacular sea life found there.

CRABS

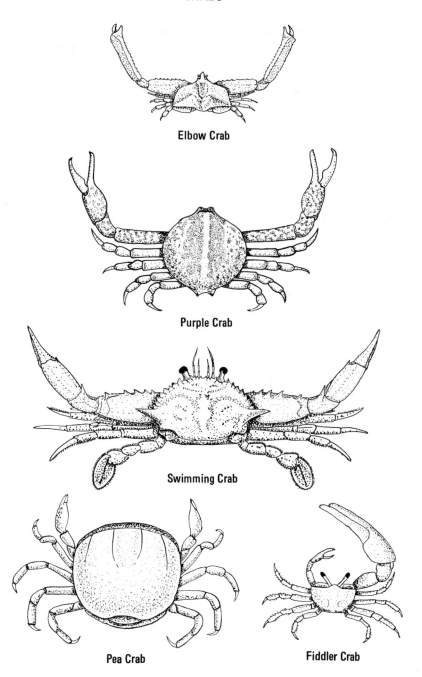

Elbow Crab

Purple Crab

Swimming Crab

Pea Crab

Fiddler Crab

CRABS

SPINY MOLE CRAB, *Blepharipoda occidentalis* Randall, 1839. It attains the greatest size of the sand crabs with a carapace length of two inches. They live together with the common sand crab but this larger one is by no means abundant. It is light blue-gray. RANGE: Stinson Beach, Marin County into lower California. LOCAL DISTRIBUTION: Sandy beaches along the coast.

MOLE CRAB or COMMON SAND CRAB, *Emerita analoga* (Stimpson, 1857). The presence of the common sand crab is shown by a characteristic V-shaped ripple in the sand after a wave moves back to the sea. This is caused by the protruding eyes and antennae. The mole crab is yellowish brown or gray and over an inch long. RANGE: Alaska to central South America. LOCAL DISTRIBUTION: In sandy beaches along open coasts.

LUMPY CRAB, *Paraxanthias taylori* (Stimpson, 1860). The chelipeds or claws and the carapace or back are particularly tuberculate or bumpy. The animal is dull red with black fingers on the claws. It attains a carapace width of more than an inch. RANGE: Monterey Bay, California, to lower Baja California Sur. LOCAL DISTRIBUTION: In rocky crevices and other secretive places along the coast.

MOTTLED PEA CRAB, *Opisthopus transversus* Rathbun, 1893. An interesting point about pea crabs is that the females live inside other animals. For example, if it is in the digestive tract of the sea cucumber it does no harm. In this situation it is known as a commensal or "mess-mate." The males are free swimming and are seldom seen. The polished surface of this crab has reddish lines and spots on a light background. The female has a width across the back of three-fourths inch, and males one-half inch in width. RANGE: Southern California. LOCAL DISTRIBUTION: In the sea cucumber, *Parastichopus*; in the siphons of piddocks, *Pholas;* in the mantle cavities of several clams; the opisthobranch, *Bulla,* keyhole limpets, *Megathura,* and between the lateral flaps of *Navanax*.

There are male crabs and female crabs. If you look underneath the crab's body, you will see that the abdomen will be folded under the central part of the body. If this sectioned or segmented flap is broad, covering most of the underside, it will be a female crab. If this segmented part is narrow at the center of the undersurface, the crab will be a male. The eggs are carried in the broad abdominal area of the female when eggs are to be hatched. She will carry them there until they hatch into baby crabs called zoa.

40

CRABS

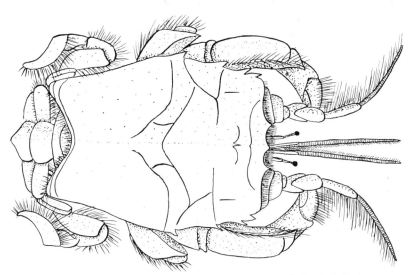

Spiny Mole Crab

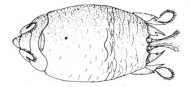

Mole Crab

Lumpy Crab

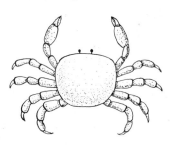

Mottled Pea Crab

CLAMS / BIVALVES

SAN DIEGO SCALLOP, *Pecten diegensis* Dall, 1898. Fossil representatives of this pecten or scallop can be found in the Pleistocene fossils at Pacific Beach. The present day San Diego scallop lives below the low tide line and occasionally is washed ashore during a storm. It is red-brown and the arched valve may be white or yellow. One valve (shell) is flattened, and the other convex. It attains a size of about four and three-fourths inches. RANGE: Bodega Bay to Cabo San Lucas, Baja California Sur. LOCAL DISTRIBUTION: Generally found in deeper water but occasionally shells are washed ashore at Coronado and the Silver Strand.

DOTTED PANDORA, *Pandora punctata* Conrad, 1837. The valves are laterally flattened with slight curvature. The inner side of the valves are pearly white and the outer side, white. It attains a length of about two inches. RANGE: Vancouver Island to the Gulf of California. LOCAL DISTRIBUTION: Sandy bottoms off shore.

BEAN CLAM, *Donax gouldii* Dall, 1921. At times the sandy beach will be covered with thousands upon thousands of bean clams. The bean clam is about an inch long, varying in color pattern but generally cream with purple-black markings. Often the clam is bearded with a tuft of hydroids (*Clytia bakeri* Torrey, 1904), a colonial coelenterate. RANGE: Santa Cruz, California, to southern Baja California. LOCAL DISTRIBUTION: Sandy beaches along the open coast.

BROAD-EARED SCALLOP, *Leptopecten latiauratus* (Conrad, 1837). The broad-eared scallop attaches itself to the surface of rocks and algae by means of thin threads. When not attached, it can swim by "jet propulsion", snapping the valves of the shell rapidly together. It is light orange-brown and about an inch long. RANGE: Marin County, California, to Cabo San Lucas and the Gulf of California. LOCAL DISTRIBUTION: On kelp washed ashore, on eel grass and algae in bays and kelp beds, and occasionally on floats.

The shipworm or "termite of the sea" is a clam. It has an affinity for untreated wood. The exterior of the wood may have many small holes in it, from which feeding siphons extend. Inside the wood in cross sections will show larger tunnels that the clam occupies. As it grows to an adult shipworm, the tube is enlarged but not so as to break into the chambers of the next shipworm. The piece of wood might be riddled with holes with little or no wood left inside. Wood is usually treated with creosote or oil-like products under pressure to extend the life of the wood in salt water.

42

CLAMS

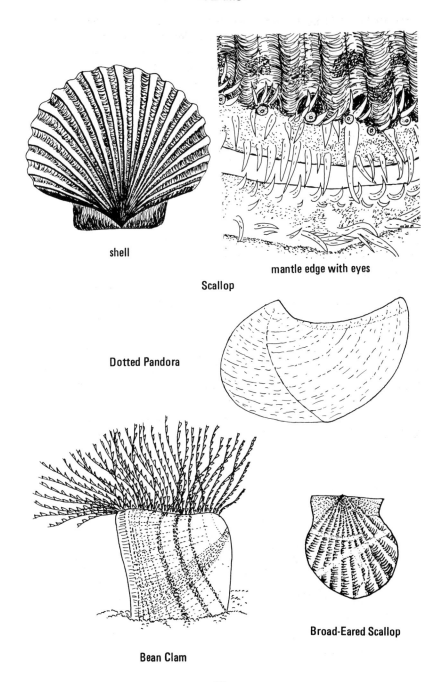

shell

mantle edge with eyes

Scallop

Dotted Pandora

Bean Clam

Broad-Eared Scallop

43

BIVALVES

CALIFORNIA MUSSEL, *Mytilus californianus* Conrad, 1837. The california mussel shell has a tough brown-black chitonous covering, which may be worn off in places to expose a purple-black and white shell. It is commonly four inches long, rarely as much as eight inches. RANGE: Alaska to Mexico. LOCAL DISTRIBUTION: On rocky headlands and on pier pilings.

BAY MUSSEL, *Mytilus edulis* Linnaeus, 1758. The bay mussel lives in quiet waters, in contrast to the california mussel, which lives on the open coast. The shell of the bay mussel is about four inches long, smooth, and black. RANGE: Around the world in north temperate seas; on this coast from Alaska to southern Baja California. LOCAL DISTRIBUTION: On wharf pilings, floats, and rocks in bays.

PLATFORM MUSSEL, *Septifer bifurcatus* (Conrad, 1837). This mussel is a solitary mussel found under rocks. It is also known as the branch-ribbed mussel because of the numerous ribs on the shell. It sometimes attains a length of two inches. It is purple-black, sometimes with white eroded areas. RANGE: Northern California to the Gulf of California. LOCAL DISTRIBUTION: Under rocks along the coast.

FAT HORSE MUSSEL, *Modiolus capax* (Conrad, 1837). Part of the fat horse mussel is bearded and covered with a brown epidermis. It attains a length of about three inches. RANGE: Santa Cruz to Peru. LOCAL DISTRIBUTION: Common on Mission Bay jetties or along rocky coasts.

DATE MUSSEL, *Lithophaga plumula* (Hanley, 1843). The date mussel is cylindrical, bluntly rounded on one end and pointedly rounded on the other. The mussel is brown and sometimes attains a length of three and one-half inches. RANGE: Mendocino County to Peru. LOCAL DISTRIBUTION: In mudstone and sandstone along the coast.

One way to tell when an ebb tide or low tide is pending is to note the condition of the moon. A full moon signifies the lowest low of the bi-weekly tides. The new or dark moon shows that the tide is perhaps half as low; low enough to discover some higher zoned organisms. Half moons signify that the tides are not low enough to stand in the intertidal.

44

MUSSELS / BIVALVES

California Mussel

Bay Mussel   Platform Mussel

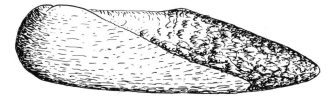

Fat Horse Mussel

Date Mussel

BIVALVES

ROUGH PEA-POD ROCK-BORER, *Adula falcata* (Gould, 1851). Although long and narrow, this bivalve is a mussel. The shell is textured and covered with a chestnut brown epidermis. It lives in mudstone or sandstone rock and can be found by breaking the rock. It attains a length of three and three-fourth inches. RANGE: Oregon to Baja California. LOCAL DISTRIBUTION: Rocky beaches.

THE LITTLE PIDDOCK, *Penitella conradi* Valenciennes, 1846. The little piddock is found burrowed into the shells of abalone and mussels. The abalone often forms blister pearls to protect itself from the burrowing piddock. The posterior part of this piddock is somewhat flattened. The little piddock attains a length of one-half inch. Its color is off-white. RANGE: British Columbia into Baja California. LOCAL DISTRIBUTION: In the shells of the abalone *Haliotis* and occasionally the mussel *Mytilus*.

SCALE-SIDED PIDDOCK, *Parapholas californica* (Conrad, 1837). The piddock is rounded posteriorly tapering anteriorly. There is a triangular shaped rough area near the posterior half of the valves. The anterior part of the shell is scaly appearing. There is a slight gap where the siphons protrude. The piddock is off-white and slightly tan and darker brown anteriorly. It reaches a length of three inches. RANGE: Bodega Bay into Baja California. LOCAL DISTRIBUTION: In soft siltstone or sandstone-like rock along the coast. It is detected by the presence of a hole in the rock.

WART-NECKED PIDDOCK, *Chaceia ovoidea* (Gould, 1851). A large shell that is gaping at both ends. The posterior part of the shell has a rib projecting into the interior of the shell. The animal burrows by moving the valves of the shell. It attains a length of four inches. The bivalve is off-white and white inside. RANGE: Santa Cruz to Bahía San Bartolome, Baja California Sur. LOCAL DISTRIBUTION: In hard clay or shale.

ROUGH PIDDOCK, *Zirfaea pilsbryi* Lowe, 1931. The posterior part of the valves are rough with pointed spines. The shell is gaping at both ends. The shell is chalky off-white and white inside. A pair of ribs project into the interior part of the bivalve. The rough piddock attains a length of four and one-half inches. RANGE: Alaska to southern Baja. LOCAL DISTRIBUTION: In heavy clay along the coast and detectable by the presence of small circular holes in the clay.

Bat rays grow to 150 pounds and 4 feet from side to side. These fish will sit on the bottom of the sand or mud and flap their fins to dig a hole in order to reach clams. The clams are crushed with pavement-like flat teeth. The holes left in the sand may cause a swimmer to suddenly drop into one and stumble; some legs have been broken this way.

BIVALVES

Rough Pea-Pod Rock Borer

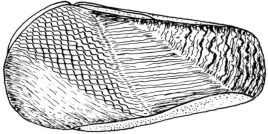

Scale-Sided Piddock

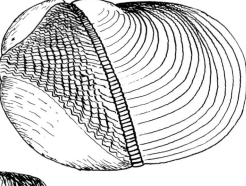

The Little Piddock

Wart-Necked Piddock

Rough Piddock

47

BIVALVES

FLAT-TIPPED PIDDOCK, *Penitella penita* (Conrad, 1837). This clam lives in burrows in rocks. It is enlarged and rounded anteriorly and smaller posteriorly. There is a triangular plate over the area of the hinge. The bivalve is off-white. It attains a length of three inches. RANGE: Alaska into Baja California. LOCAL DISTRIBUTION: In mudstone, siltstone and sandstone along the coast.

NATIVE OYSTER, *Ostrea lurida* Carpenter, 1864. The native oyster is not very symmetrical; it may be circular or elongated, nearly flat or bent. It is generally off-white and up to two inches wide. Oysters are good to eat and are cultivated in northern bays and sloughs. RANGE: Sitka, Alaksa, to Cabo San Lucas, Baja California Sur. LOCAL DISTRIBUTION: In San Diego and Mission Bays and on rocks and pilings.

WAVY CHIONE or HARD-SHELL COCKLE, *Chione undatella* (Sowerby, 1835). The wavy chione can be found alive only by digging in the mudflats, though the empty shells can be found on the shores of the bay. The shell is yellow-white and about two and one-fourth inches wide. California fishing laws state that animals less than one and one-half inches cannot be taken. RANGE: Santa Barbara County, California, to Peru. LOCAL DISTRIBUTION: In the sandy mudflats of bays.

WHITE SEA COCKLE, *Amiantis callosa* (Conrad, 1837). The sea cockle is a heavy glossy-white shell with concentric ridges. The interior of the shell is chalky-white. The white sea cockle attains a length of five inches. RANGE: Santa Barbara to Mexico. LOCAL DISTRIBUTION: Under the breaker line of sandy beaches. Occasionally washes ashore after a storm.

The mussel hangs onto the rocky substrate with byssal filaments to prevent waves from dislodging them during the waves at high tide. The waves flow across the shell; the shells agape to let water in so as to feed upon detritus, diatoms (one-celled plants) and zooplankton (small animals). This is done by a filtration process. The California mussel is the largest here and needs open coastal wave action. The bays have bay mussels, a smaller broader type that occur between rocks and under rocks. Wild mussels have open and closed seasons to protect people who eat them from the toxins in the gut of the mussel. A sea star will pull at the two valves with tube feet in order to weaken the adductor muscle so the valve gapes. The sea star will evert its stomach into the shell and digest the mussel in the shell. When finished, the two valves of the mussel are abandoned.

BIVALVES

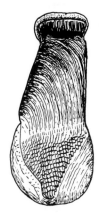

Flat-Tipped Piddock

Native Oyster

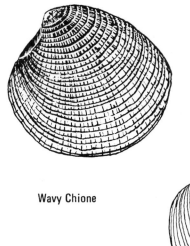

Wavy Chione

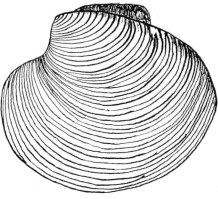

White Sea Cockle

MARINE SNAILS - PROSOBRANCHIA

The phylum Mollusca includes clams, snails, and octopuses. With some 60,000 kinds, mollusks are second only to th arthropods in numbers of species. They are soft-bodied, mostly with hard shells, but their shells and bodies are reletively massive and not delicately jointed like those of the arthropods. Most mollusks are marine, though some clams and many snails live in fresh water and many snails live on land.

The mollusks fall into six classes, four of which are represented in this guide. The pelecypods or bivalves, such as clams and mussels, have two shells, or valves, hinged at the top, and an axe-shaped foot which many of them use for digging their way into sand or mud. The gastropods, such as snails and slugs, usually have a single spirally coiled shell but may have none. The chitons have a shell of eight separate overlapping plates in a row. Most modern cephalopods, such as the octopuses and squids, have no external shell; they have eight or ten arms, with suction discs.

FILE LIMPET, *Collisella limatula* (Carpenter, 1864). The file limpet has coarse ribs like the teeth of a file. The shell is over an inch long, tan or gray—green outside, white inside with black around the edge. RANGE: Oregon to southern Baja California Sur. LOCAL DISTRIBUTION: In the high tide area of the rocky shore.

ROUGH LIMPET, *Collisella scabra* (Gould, 1846). The rough limpet is characteristically deeply scalloped along the edge and ribbed along the sides. It is relatively flat and measures up to an inch long. It is generally light tan. RANGE: Oregon to southern Baja California. LOCAL DISTRIBUTION: On and under rocks.

RIBBED LIMPET, *Collisella digitalis* (Rathke, 1833). The ribbed limpet is rough textured, with a varied pattern becasue of erosion. It is generally greenish-tan or grayish and may be an inch long. RANGE: Aleutian Islands, Alaska, to southern Baja California. LOCAL DISTRIBUTION: Collected in clusters in the high tide area on rocky surfaces generally about rocks.

SEAWEED LIMPET, *Notoacmea insessa* (Hinds, 1842). The seaweed limpet grows on the stipe (stem) of the feather boa (*Egregia*, a brown alga) and apparently is limited to this habitat. The red-brown shell is smooth and about three-fourths inch long. RANGE: Alaska to Bahía Magdalena, Baja California Sur. LOCAL DISTRIBUTION: On the brown alga *Egregia*.

OWL LIMPET, *Lottis gigantea* Sowerby, 1834. The meat of the owl limpet is reported to be very palatable when prepared like that of abalone. The shell is up to three inches long, rough and dull brown outside, but blue-white toward the center and dark toward the edge inside. RANGE: Washington to Bahía Tortugas, Baja California Sur. LOCAL DISTRIBUTION: Common in the high tide area of rocky beaches, when not overcollected by humans.

LIMPETS

VOLCANO KEYHOLE LIMPET, *Fissurella volcano* Reeve, 1849. This limpet is generally oval with an oblong "keyhole" at the center, suggesting the shape of a volcano. It is ashy-pink with 13 to 16 purple rays and may be an inch long. RANGE: Crescent City, California, to Bahía Magdalena, Baja California Sur. LOCAL DISTRIBUTION: In the high tide zone on rocks.

GIANT KEYHOLE LIMPET, *Megathura crenulata* (Sowerby, 1825). The giant keyhole limpet is oblong and massive, sometimes seven inches long. The foot of the living animal is orange-yellow. The shell is nearly covered by a black or tan mantle, as is the "keyhole." RANGE: Monterey, California, to Isla Asuncion, Baja California Sur. LOCAL DISTRIBUTION: On jetties and rocks along the coast.

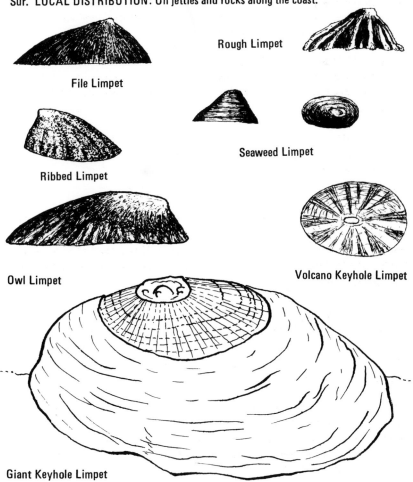

File Limpet

Rough Limpet

Ribbed Limpet

Seaweed Limpet

Owl Limpet

Volcano Keyhole Limpet

Giant Keyhole Limpet

WHITE CAP LIMPET, *Acmaea mitra* Rathke, 1833. The white cap limpet is usually found with encrusting algae on it; however when the algae is removed, the shell is white inside and outside. It is a steep conical shell with the point near the center of the shell. The shell otherwise is generally smooth. It attains a size of one and one-half inches long and one and one-fourth inches high. RANGE: Alaska to northern Baja California. LOCAL DISTRIBUTION: Subtidal, occasionally washed ashore after a storm.

RIBBED HOOFSNAIL, *Hipponix tumens* Carpenter, 1864. The apex instead of being at the top of the shell is off center near the end of the shell. The surface of the shell is covered with small radial and concentric ridges. The ribbed hoofsnail attains a length of about three-fourths inch. The shell is white with brown beard-like hairs near the margin. RANGE: Crescent City, California, to Bahía Magdalena, Baja California Sur LOCAL DISTRIBUTION: About rocks at low tide along the coast.

PAINTED LIMPET, *Notoacmea dipicta* (Hinds, 1842). A very narrow, oblong shell particularly suited to its habitat of living on the blades of eelgrass. It is a tan shell with red-brown radiating lines. The apex of the shell is near the posterior end of the shell. It is one-half inch long, one-eighth inch wide and three-sixteenths inch high. RANGE: San Pedro to southern Baja California. LOCAL DISTRIBUTION: It lives on the eelgrass found in bays. With the continuing "development" of southern California bays, it is in danger of elimination.

NEAT-RIB KEYHOLE LIMPET, *Diodora arnoldi* McLean, 1966. This keyhole limpet is tan with about 12 radiating dark brown rays. The opening in the top of the shell is not at the center but located posteriorly, the anterior portion being slightly curved and expanded. The inside of the shell is white. It attains a length of three-fourths inch. RANGE: Crescent City, California, to San Martin, Island, Baja California Norte. LOCAL DISTRIBUTION: Rocky areas below the low tide line.

CALIFORNIA CAECUM, *Caecum californicum* Dall, 1885. Although this animal is somewhat common, it is difficult to see because of its size. It has a small white shell that is slightly curved, tapering and with a number of rings. It attains a length of one-eighth inch. RANGE: Monterey to Bahía Magdalena, Baja California Sur. LOCAL DISTRIBUTION: In gravel under rocks and sublittoral.

Pier pilings, jetties, boat bottoms, ropes in the water are places to find some types of sea life.

SNAIL SHELLS

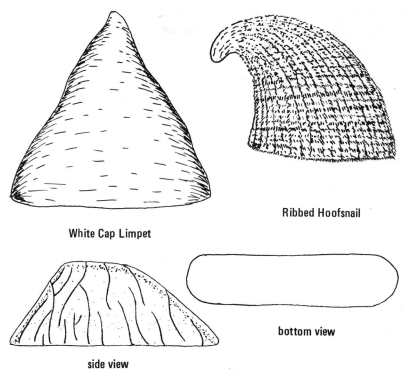

White Cap Limpet

Ribbed Hoofsnail

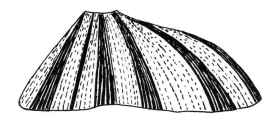

side view

bottom view

Painted Limpet

Neat-rib Keyhole Limpet

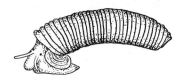

California Caecum

SNAIL SHELLS

CATALINA TROPHON, *Trophon cerrosensis catalinensis* Oldroyd, 1927. There are seven thin-edged varices projecting from the delicate shell. This trophon attains a height of two to three inches. It is pale tan. RANGE: Southern California. LOCAL DISTRIBUTION: Deep water off shore.

BELCHER'S MUREX SHELL, *Forreria belcheri* (Hinds, 1844). The opening to the shell is relatively large with a tooth on the edge of the aperture. The belcher's murex attains a length of six inches. It is tannish or lighter. RANGE: Mugu Lagoon to central Baja California. LOCAL DISTRIBUTION: Mission Bay and in deeper water off the coast. It is rare.

THREE-WINGED MUREX, *Pteropurpura trialata* (Sowerby, 1841). The shell has three prominent varices about three-fourths of an inch high projecting from it. The three-winged murex attains a length of four inches. It is creamy white or white with dark brown bands. Sometimes it has nearly completely dark brown bands, and sometimes the shell is nearly completely dark brown. RANGE: Bodega Bay, California, to central Baja California. LOCAL DISTRIBUTION: Intertidal on rocky coasts.

CALIFORNIA FROGSNAIL, *Bursa californica* (Hinds, 1843). The California frogsnail is a rather heavy bodied shell with a large opening for the animal. It attains a length of six inches but is usually smaller. It is a creamy white or light tan, fresh specimens have four light brown bands. RANGE: Monterey Bay to Gulf of California. LOCAL DISTRIBUTION: San Diego and Mission Bays, tide pools occasionally and off shore.

There are phosphorescent and luminescent micro- and macro-organisms such as one-celled animals with a flagellum, segmented annelid worms, sea pansies and midshipmen fish with light organs called photophores. During plankton blooms or red tides, the waves in the dark of the night glow with a blue-green light. If, on a dark night at the beach, you look into the footsteps you have just made in the wet beach or bay sand, you may see small bright spots of light caused by the agitation of the small luminescent organisms. Luminescent worms also occur at the beach. In the boat harbor of Chula Vista next to the breakwater, when conditions are right, luminescent segmented worms can be seen doing whirligigs at the surface.

54

SNAIL SHELLS

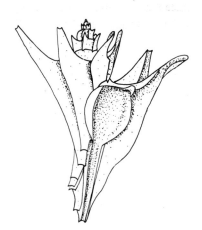

Catalina Trophon

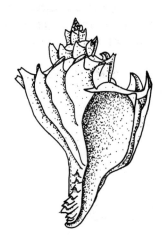

Belcher's Murex

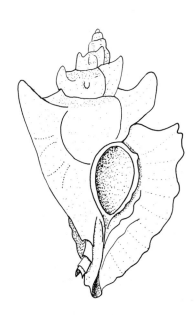

Three-Winged Murex

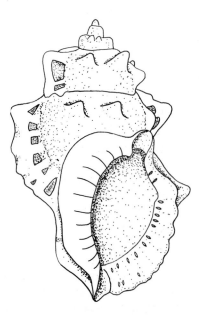

California Frogsnail

NORRIS' TOPSNAIL, *Norrisia norrisi* (Sowerby, 1838). Norris' topsnail is about two inches wide. The shell is rich brown, and the living animal is a bright red. RANGE: Point Conception, California, to Isla Asuncion, Baja California Sur. LOCAL DISTRIBUTION: On brown algae of the Mission Bay jetties and about rocks at very low tide along the coast.

BLACK TEGULA, *Tegula funebralis* (A. Adams, 1955). The black tegula or black turban is one of the first animals found at the rocky beach. It hides under rocks during the day and comes out at night. The shell is black, often with a purple tinge, although the top is usually worn away exposing a white surface. It commonly reaches almost an inch in diameter. RANGE: Vancouver Island, British Columbia, to central Baja California. LOCAL DISTRIBUTION: Upper tidal zone in rocky areas.

WESTERN BANDED TEGULA, *Tegula eiseni* Jordan, 1936. The shell is generally found lower on the beach than the black tegula. It is less than an inch high. It is brown; its beaded lines spotted with black. RANGE: Los Angeles County, California, to Bahía Magdalena, Baja California Sur. LOCAL DISTRIBUTION: In the medium-low tide area of rock shores.

WAVY TURBAN, *Astraea undosa* (Wood, 1828). Wavy turban shells are conical and often more than four inches wide. The under surface is pearly, and the sides are covered with a fibrous brown epidermis giving it a rough appearance. Often the shell is covered with algae and hydroids. The operculum or "door" is thick and has two prominent curved ridges. RANGE: Point Conception, California, to Isla Asuncion, Baja California Sur. LOCAL DISTRIBUTION: On rocky beaches and jetties.

RED TURBAN, *Astraea gibberosa* (Dillwyn, 1817). Red turban is often mistaken for the wavy turban. It can easily be distinguished by the operculum which is thick and rounded, without the prominent ridges or ribs of the wavy turban. The shell is brick-red. It attains a diameter of two and one-half inches. RANGE: Vancouver to Bahía Magdalena. LOCAL DISTRIBUTION: Rarely found washed ashore after a storm. Rock areas.

QUEEN TEGULA, *Tegula regina* (Stearns, 1892). The queen tegula is a handsome conical shell with low ridges radiating down the shell. The shell is purple-black or brown and at times covered with encrusting algae. The area around the opening to the shell is orange and pearly white. The queen tegula attains a height of two inches and a diameter of about two inches. RANGE: Catalina Island to Isla Asuncion Sur. LOCAL DISTRIBUTION: Subtidal rocky areas, jetty or Mission Bay and Coronados Islands, Baja California Norte.

SNAIL SHELLS

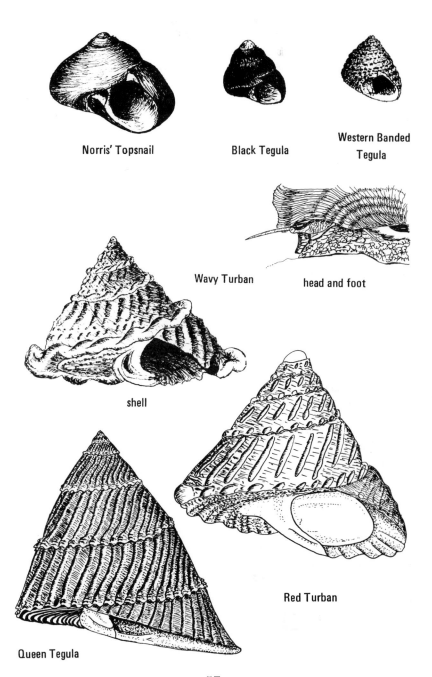

Norris' Topsnail

Black Tegula

Western Banded
Tegula

Wavy Turban

head and foot

shell

Queen Tegula

Red Turban

SNAIL SHELLS

GEMMED TOP SHELL, *Calliostoma gemmulatum* Carpenter, 1864. The gemmed top shell is finely beaded on the ridges of the shell. The shell is light brown with vertical irregular banding; beads are light green. It attains a diameter of one-half and three-fourth inches. RANGE: Monterey to Baja California Sur. LOCAL DISTRIBUTION: Rocky coasts and estuaries.

PURPLE-RINGED TOP SHELL,*Calliostoma annulatum* (Lightfoot, 1786). This top shell is strikingly marked by a purple band at the sutures on a bright golden yellow background. The surface of the shell is finely beaded. It attains a diameter of about an inch. RANGE: Alaska into Baja California. LOCAL DISTRIBUTION: Deep water; at times washed ashore.

CHANNELED TOP SHELL, *Calliostoma canaliculatum* (Lightfoot, 1786). This top shell is slightly larger than the ringed top shell. The spiral ridges of this shell contains little or no beading as is the case in the ringed top shell. The channeled top shell attains a diameter of a little better than an inch and a half. The shell is light brown with white ridges. RANGE: Alaska to Camalu, Baja California Norte. LOCAL DISTRIBUTION: On kelp holdfasts, occasionally washed ashore and in deep water.

THREE COLORED TOP SHELL, *Calliostoma tricolor* Gabb, 1865. This top shell differs from the other three by having alternating dashes of purple and white. The shell has many finely beaded ridges as in the ringed top shell. It attains a diameter of about three-fourths inch. RANGE: Santa Cruz to Isla San Martin, Baja California Norte. LOCAL DISTRIBUTION: San Diego Bay.

PURPLE DWARF OLIVE, *Olivella biplicata* (Sowerby, 1825). This olive snail can be detected in its home under the sand by a depressed trail. Digging in the sand at the end of the trail will usually produce the snail. The shell is highly polished, white and purplish, and up to three-fourths of an inch long. RANGE: Vancouver Island, British Columbia, to Bahía Magdalena, Baja California Sur. LOCAL DISTRIBUTION: In sandy areas of bays and the San Diego river flood control channel.

San Diego exported 1,160 metric tons of edible products of fishery items in 1982. This included sea urchins, 17,229,000 pounds; abalone, 1,095 pounds; spiny lobster, 479,000 pounds; squid, 35,803,000 pounds; and anchovies, 103,300,000 pounds. Source: Lipow & Fay, 1984/85. California Almanac.

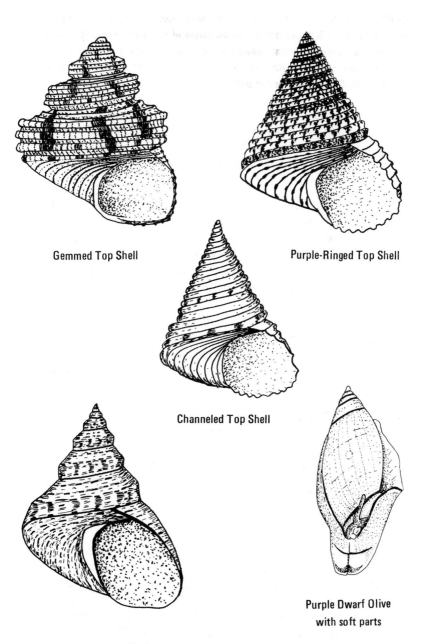

Gemmed Top Shell

Purple-Ringed Top Shell

Channeled Top Shell

Tricolor Top Shell

Purple Dwarf Olive
with soft parts

SNAIL SHELLS

ERODED PERIWINKLE or GRAY LITTORINE, *Littorina planaxis* Philippi, 1847. Among the limpets and barnacles of the spray area great numbers of the eroded periwinkle can be found. It can be found as much as 20 feet above high tide. The dingy, gray shell may be three-fourths inch high. The inner margin of the opening is large and flattened. RANGE: Oregon to Bahía Magdalena, Baja California. LOCAL DISTRIBUTION: In the spray area on rocky cliffs along the coast.

CHECKERED PERIWINKLE, *Littorina scutulata* Gould, 1849. The checkered periwinkle occurs only a few feet above the high tide line. It is smaller and slimmer than the eroded periwinkle (about one-fourth inch) and lacks the flattened area. It is brown or black, checkered with white. RANGE: Alaska to Bahía Tortugas, Baja California Sur. LOCAL DISTRIBUTION: Along the rocky cliffs of our coast.

ONYX SLIPPER SNAIL, *Crepidula onyx* Sowerby, 1824. The onyx slippersnail can be found as many as three deep, one on top of the other. It is light brown and may be two inches long. The inner side of the shell has a white shelf. RANGE: Monterey, California, to Chile. LOCAL DISTRIBUTION: On rocks and on other shells in bays where there is mud.

SPINY CUP-AND-SAUCER, *Crucibulum spinosum* (Sowerby, 1824). The outer surface of this shell may or may not contain many spine-like projections. Inside there is a small cup. The cup-and-saucer limpet attains a diameter of about an inch. This limpet is almost white. RANGE: California to Chile. LOCAL DISTRIBUTION: On stones and backs of shells in San Diego and Mission Bays.

RECLUZ'S MOONSNAIL, *Polinices reclusiana* (Deshayes, 1839). A particularly interesting fact about the recluz's moonsnail is that it mixes sand and eggs together into a sand-colored egg "collar" formed around its very large foot. The shell itself is a rich tan and may be two inches wide. RANGE: Mugu Lagoon, California, to Mazatlan, Mexico. LOCAL DISTRIBUTION: In San Diego and Mission Bays on muddy sand.

A moon snail lays its countless minute eggs mixed in a gelatin-like substance and grains of sand forming a thin circular ribbon known as an egg collar. The circular form may overlap.

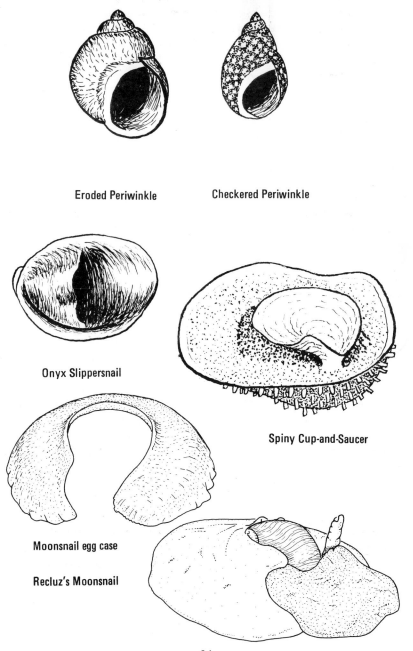

Eroded Periwinkle   Checkered Periwinkle

Onyx Slippersnail

Spiny Cup-and-Saucer

Moonsnail egg case

Recluz's Moonsnail

SNAIL SHELLS

SOLANDER'S TRIVIA, *Trivia solandri* (Sowerby, 1832). The shape of this shell is similar to that of a cowry. There are numerous light-colored ridges on the shell ending in white knobs at the top of the shell. The shell can range in color from brown through pink. It attains a length of three-fourths inch. RANGE: Palos Verdes, Los Angeles County, California, to Panama. LOCAL DISTRIBUTION: Rocky areas along the coast.

CHESTNUT COWRY, *Cypraea spadicea* Swainson, 1823. The chestnut cowry is a highly polished shell that is white below with a brown area at the top of the shell. It attains a length of two inches. RANGE: Monterey to Isla Cedros, Baja California Sur. LOCAL DISTRIBUTION: Rocky areas intertidal and subtidal. Although not particularly uncommon, it seems to be limited to Point Loma where it is protected from being collected.

LEWIS MOONSNAIL, *Polinices lewisii* (Gould, 1847). When the foot is fully extended, it hardly seems possible that it could be pulled into the shell and the operculum closed behind it. It is the largest of the moonsnails, attaining a length of four inches. The shell is a brown-white. RANGE: British Columbia to Baja California. LOCAL DISTRIBUTION: On mudflats in bays and in deeper water off our coast.

CALIFORNIA CONE, *Conus californicus* Reeve, 1844. The California cone has a conical shell about an inch long, upturned at the end of the long, narrow aperture. It is a flat brown when alive. RANGE: Farallon Islands, California, to Bahía Magdalena, Baja California Sur. LOCAL DISTRIBUTION: On rocky beaches and the flood control channel of the San Diego River.

BLACK ABALONE, *Haliotis cracherodii* Leach, 1814. The black abalone is smooth, green-black, and up to ten inches in length. It has five to nine openings near the edge of its shell for the passage of water after the oxygen has been extracted by the gills. RANGE: Coos Bay, Oregon, to Cabo San Lucas, Baja California Sur. LOCAL DISTRIBUTION: Under rocks along the coast.

GREEN ABALONE, *Haliotis fulgens* Philippi, 1845. The green abalone is about 10 inches long and a red-brown color, with 30 or 40 spiral ridges, and with 5 or 6 small slightly elevated circular openings along its edge. It is relatively low and flattened compared to the other abalones, which tend to be deeper bodied. RANGE: Point Conception, California, to Bahía Magdalena, Baja California Sur. LOCAL DISTRIBUTION: Found in rocky intertidal areas usually at the low tide level.

It is known that birds of a feather flock together.

SNAIL SHELLS

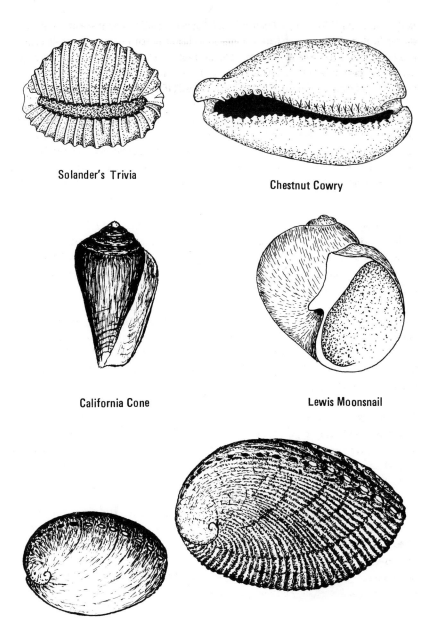

Solander's Trivia

Chestnut Cowry

California Cone

Lewis Moonsnail

Green Abalone

Black Abalone

SNAIL SHELLS

LIVID MACRON, *Macron lividus* (A. Adams, 1855). The livid macron has a thick shell about an inch long. It has a dark brown epidermis when alive. RANGE: Orange County, California, to Bahía San Bartolome, Baja California Sur. LOCAL DISTRIBUTION: Under rocks intertidally along the coast.

NUTTALL HORNMOUTH, *Ceratostoma nuttallii* (Conrad, 1837). The shell has a sharp horn at the outer edge of the opening, whence the name. It is commonly about one and one-half inches long, but may reach two inches. It is white or brown, or a mixture of both colors. The shell is generally rather lumpy. RANGE: Point Conception, California, to Baja California. LOCAL DISTRIBUTION: On the Mission Bay jetties and other rocky areas.

ANGULAR UNICORN, *Acanthina spirata* (Blainville, 1832). The shell of the angular unicorn is about one and one-fourth inches long, with a small sharp horn at the opening. Near the opening there are 10 or 12 light colored lines, with dark markings which give the shell a checkered appearance. RANGE: Tomales Bay, California, to Camalu, Baja California Norte. LOCAL DISTRIBUTION: On rocky jetties and rocks near the upper tide zone.

CALIFORNIA MARGINELLA or "WHEAT SHELL," *Volvarina taeniolata* Mörch, 1860. The California Marginella has a highly polished smooth shell. As many as six or seven may sometimes be found under a single rock. It is pale yellow-white with a dark central band. RANGE: Point Conception, California, to Ecuador. LOCAL DISTRIBUTION: Under rocks along the coast.

CALIFORNIA HORN SHELL, *Cerithidea californica* (Haldeman, 1840). During a minus tide, the California horn shell can be found in great numbers on mud flats. It is dark brown or sometimes almost black and over an inch and a half long. RANGE: Bolinas Bay, California, to Laguna San Ignacio, Baja California Sur. LOCAL DISTRIBUTION: On the mud flats of Mission and San Diego Bays.

SCALED WORM SHELL, *Serpulorbis squamigerus* (Carpenter, 1857). This interesting snail generally attaches itself to a rock and grows like a tubeworm, for which it can be mistaken. It generally grows in clusters of several individuals. The shell is several inches long and whitish, but the exposed part of the animal is almost black. RANGE: Santa Barbara, California, to Baja California. LOCAL DISTRIBUTION: Near the edge under rocks in the medium tide zone.

The Pacific Ocean is 64,186,000 square miles with an average depth of 12,925 feet.

SNAIL SHELLS

Livid Macron

Nuttall Hornmouth

California Marginella

Angular Unicorn

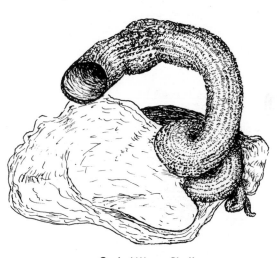

California Horn Shell

Scaled Worm Shell

SNAIL SHELLS

OREGON TRITON, *Fusitriton oregonensis* (Redfield, 1847). The shell of this triton is covered with a hairy brown epidermis. The area around the opening to the shell is white. The hairy Oregon triton attains a length of five inches. RANGE: Alaska to La Jolla. LOCAL DISTRIBUTON: Deep water offshore.

CARPENTER'S TURRID, *Megasurcula carpenteriana* (Gabb, 1865). The opening to this shell is one half the length of the shell. Carpenter's turrid is light brown with darker striping, some are red-brown. The opening to the shell is cream colored. Carpenter's Turrid attains a length of four inches. RANGE: Bodega Bay to Baja California. LOCAL DISTRIBUTION: Deep water and rocky shores.

IDA'S MITER, *Mitra idae* Melville, 1893. The ida's miter is smooth. It is covered with a black epidermis, and the area around the opening to the shell is white. At times it attains a length of tree inches. RANGE: Crescent City, California, to Isla Cedros, Baja California Norte. LOCAL DISTRIBUTION: Deep water and rocky shores.

DANA AUGUR SHELL, *Terebra danai* Berry, 1958. There are about 12 whorls on the shell. The aperture to the shell is elongated. The dana augur shell is elongated and is yellow-brown with an interior of brown. It attains a length of one and one-fourth inches. RANGE: Southern California. LOCAL DISTRIBUTION: Deeper water, occasionally washed ashore in great numbers.

LEAN WESTERN NASSA, *Nassarius mendicus* (Gould, 1849). It attains a length of one-half inch. The shell is rusty brown with a light white interior. There are knobby ridges next to spiraling grooves. RANGE: Alaska to Isla Asuncion, Baja California Sur. LOCAL DISTRIBUTION: Subtidal in San Diego and Mission Bays.

Rachel Carlson in her book Silent Spring drew attention to pestacides and how it affects wildlife. The now banned DDT is not biodegradable and still lingers in the ocean. It has found its way into fish and into sea birds that eat the fish, causing thin-shelled eggs when laid. The eggs are then flattened by the incubating pelican.

La Jolla Cove has a protected underwater marine park with its habitat and occupants left in quiet solitude. It is a great place to view the open-coast type of habitat and sea cliffs.

SNAIL SHELLS

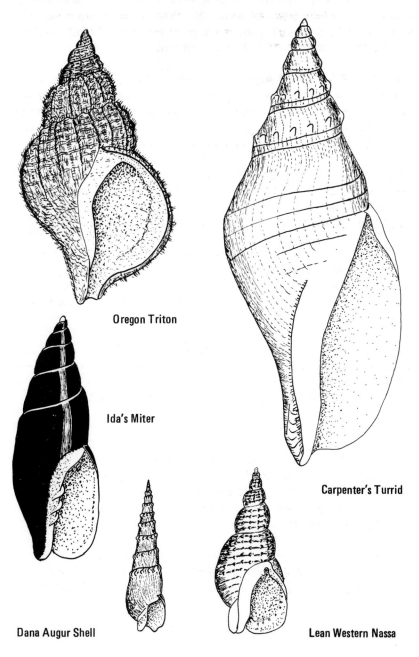

Oregon Triton

Ida's Miter

Carpenter's Turrid

Dana Augur Shell

Lean Western Nassa

SNAIL SHELLS

MONEY WENTLETRAP, *Epitonium indianorum* (Carpenter, 1865). There are deep constrictions at the junction of the whorls. The wentletrap has several prominent ribs, aligned up and down the shell. The opening to the shell is nearly round. The money wentletrap is off-white. It attains a length of an inch. RANGE: Alaska to Bahía San Quintin, Baja California Norte. LOCAL DISTRIBUTION: Deep water, 25-70 fathoms. Around rocks and sand about *Tealia*.

COOPER'S TURRET, *Turritella cooperi* Carpenter, 1864. The distinct tapering spire of this shell has faint spiral ridges. The this turret attains a length of almost two inches. The shell has a slight yellow color to it and at times has brown spots. RANGE: Monterey to Isla Cedros, Baja California Norte. LOCAL DISTRIBUTION: Sandy beaches.

LOOPING SHELL, *Truncatella californica* Pfeiffer, 1857. A very small shell with about eight whorls. The looping shell attains a length of one-half inch. The shell is light brown. RANGE: Santa Catalina Island to Bahía Magdalena. LOCAL DISTRIBUTION: Around rocks on rocky rubble beach where they are found about one and one-half feet below the surface.

PYRAMID SHELL, *Pyramidella mexicana* Dall & Bartsch, 1909. There are about ten whorls on the conical shell. The shell has a brown epidermis with a light colored encrustation on it. It attains a length of three-fourths inch. RANGE: Southern California to northern Baja California. LOCAL DISTRIBUTION: In bays and sandy areas.

BALCIS, *Balcis thersites* (Carpenter, 1864). The opening or aperture to this shell is elongate. The shell is white with a high luster. The shell attains a length of one-half inch. RANGE: Monterey, California, to Isla San Geronimo, Baja California Norte. LOCAL DISTRIBUTION: Sandy bottoms along the coast, some found on sides of sea cucumbers.

> The round sting ray has a sharp serrated-edge spine at the base of its tail that is poisonous... step upon it and a painful wound will occur. They are abundant in bays and found along sandy beaches. It may cover itself with sand awaiting a meal or simply to hide. This round sting ray may grow to 20 inches long. Swimmers should be alert for this fish.

SNAIL SHELLS

Money Wentletrap

Looping Shell

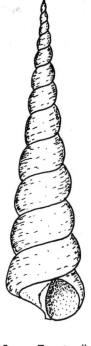

Cooper Turretsnail

Pyramid Shell

Balcis

CHITONS

MOSSY CHITON, *Mopalia muscosa* (Gould, 1846). The mossy chiton usually has encrusting plants and animals on the greenish-brown plates, causing it to blend well with its background. It reaches a length of about two inches. Along the mantle there are numerous hairy projections. RANGE: British Columbia, Canada, to Isla Cedros, Baja California Sur. LOCAL DISTRIBUTION: In deep depressions that the animal has made in the rocks.

CHITON, *Cyanoplax lowei* Pilsbry, 1918. A wide chiton that is seldom seen because of its habit. The plates are olive green, inside of the plates are white. The surface of the plates are generally smooth as is the mantle. It attains a length of about an inch. RANGE: Monterey Bay to San Diego. LOCAL DISTRIBUTION: Found in deeper water or on kelp holdfasts that have just washed ashore.

PACIFIC GLASS-HAIRED CHITON, *Acanthochitona avicula* (Carpenter, 1866). The most distinguishing point about this chiton is the presence of tufts or glass-like hairs at the corners of the over-lapping plates. The animal is light tan with or without darker markings and with or without a white line down the center. It attains a length of about an inch. RANGE: Los Angeles to the Gulf of California. LOCAL DISTRIBUTION: Specimens have been taken in Mission Bay about rocks.

BIG-END CHITON, *Callistochiton palmulatus* Pilsbry, 1893. The most distinguishing feature about this chiton is the pronounced height and shape of the tail plate; it is heavily sculptured with radiating ridges. The mantle is smooth. The inside of the plates are white. Animals are gray-tan. The big-end chiton attains a length of three-fourths of an inch. RANGE: Monterey Bay to Santo Tomas, Baja California Norte. LOCAL DISTRIBUTION: Rocky shores along the coast.

HARTWEG'S CHITON, *Cyanoplax hartwegii* (Carpenter, 1855). Hartweg's chiton is oval, somewhat flattened, and appears relatively smooth to the naked eye. It has eight olive green valves. RANGE: Monterey, California, to Punta Abreojos, Baja California Sur. LOCAL DISTRIBUTION: Found intertidally under rocks along the coast.

CONSPICUOUS CHITON, *Stenoplax conspicua* (Pilsbry, 1892). The conspicuous chiton reaches four inches in length. It is green with white and pink in the centers of the valves. RANGE: Santa Barbara County, California, to Isla Cedros, Baja California Sur. LOCAL DISTRIBUTION: Adhering to the under side of smooth rounded rocks that are partially buried in a sandy substratum often in numbers.

A sea gull will take a clam, fly with it over a parking lot and drop it to break the shells so as to feed upon it.

CHITONS

Mossy Chiton

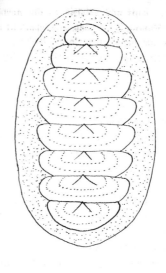

Chiton

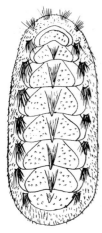

Pacific Glass-
Haired Chiton

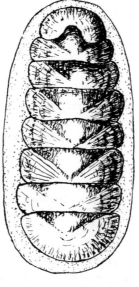

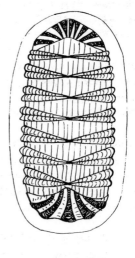

Hartweg's Chiton   Conspicuous Chiton   Big-End Chiton

71

OPISTHOBRANCHS

CALIFORNIA BUBBLE, *Bulla gouldiana* Pilsbry, 1893. This animal has an orange-yellow body and a thin shell of mottled brown sometimes two and one-half inches long. The animal burrows in sandy or muddy substrates. RANGE: Santa Barbara, California, to Mexico. LOCAL DISTRIBUTION: Abundant in San Diego and Mission Bays along the tide line.

NAVANAX, *Navanax inermis* (Cooper, 1863). The navanax is a sea slug about seven inches long with many yellow dots and a few blue dots on a brown background. It lays a light yellow stringy egg mass, which is frequently seen. When disturbed, the navanax extrudes a yellow fluid to discourage intruders. It eats various other opistho-branchs, especially *Bulla*. RANGE: Monterey Bay, California, to the Gulf of California. LOCAL DISTRIBUTION: On rocky shores and in bays. See color print at start of this book.

BARREL SHELL, *Rictaxis punctocaelatus* (Carpenter, 1864). An unusual fact about this opisthobranch is that it has an operculum. Being an opisthobranch, it is related to the bubble shells and the nudibranchs. The barrel shell has white and black banding. It attains a length of about one-half inch. RANGE: Alaska to Baja California. LOCAL DISTRIBUTION: Rocky shores along the coast.

GREEN PAPER BUBBLE, *Haminoea virescens* (Sowerby, 1833). This shell has the habit of moving along under the surface of the mud in esturies. The shell is thin and brown. The aperture is greatly enlarged at one end. It attains a length of a little over one-half inch. RANGE: Puget Sound to Mexico. LOCAL DISTRIBUTION: Found about eel grass on mud flats in estuaries.

ELYSIA, *Elysia hedgpethi* Marcus, 1961. This animal lives beautifully camouflaged on green algae. Its body color is green with minute blue flecks. It reaches a length of an inch. RANGE: From Puget Sound, Washington, to Bahía San Quintin, Baja California, and in the northern Gulf of California. LOCAL DISTRIBUTION: Principally on the green alga *Codium*.

Occasionally an orange or red-orange sea slug called *Berthellina engeli* is seen intertidally or subtidally. It has many cells in its skin containing an acid that measures a Ph 1, or the most acid in the scale from one for a very strong acid to 15 for the strongest base.

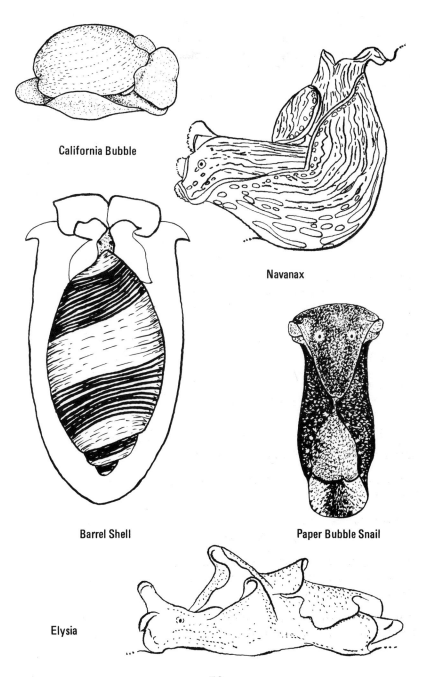

California Bubble

Navanax

Barrel Shell

Paper Bubble Snail

Elysia

OPISTHOBRANCHS

BLACK SEA HARE or COW-LIKE APLYSIA, *Aplysia vaccaria* Winkler, 1955. The cow-like aplysia is smooth and firmly muscular, as compared to the common sea hare, which is soft to the touch. It is called cow-like because of its grazing habits on the brown algae, *Egregia*, its principal food. It attains a length of more than a foot. It is deep purplish-black. RANGE: Morro Bay, California, to the Gulf of California, Baja California. LOCAL DISTRIBUTION: Common; usually scattered about the tidal flats on or between rocks.

CALIFORNIA or COMMON SEA HARE, *Aplysia californica* Cooper, 1863. The sea hare is a naked mottled brown animal up to 15 inches long. When handled, it extrudes a purple fluid into the water. Its large stringly masses of eggs are seen intermingled with algae during breeding season. RANGE: Bodega Bay, California, to the Gulf of California. LOCAL DISTRIBUTION: Common about rocks in the breeding season.

NUDIBRANCHS

Nudibranchs are colorful often elusive snails that have no shell in their adult lives. Most have a microscopic shell when the young hatch from the egg. Nudibranchs make good photographic subjects because of their varied delicate shapes and transparent, translucent or opaque coloring. Most of these animals are less than three inches. They feed upon sponges, hydroids, corals, anemones, tunicates and bryozoans, to name a few. Numerous species are represented here.

Acanthodoris rhodoceras Cockerell in Cockerell and Eliot, 1905. COLOR: It has a white base with dark papillae ringed in yellow and red. RANGE: Dillon Beach, California, to Punta Mesquite, Baja California Norte.

Trapania velox (Cockerell, 1901). COLOR: It has yellow processes and brown lines on a white body. RANGE: San Luis Obispo County to San Diego.

Atagema alba (O'Donoghue, 1927). COLOR: Dark tan with four darker tan dots. RANGE: Monterey Bay to San Diego.

Ancula lentiginosa Farmer in Farmer and Sloan, 1964. COLOR: The white base has scattered brick red markings. RANGE: Monterey to La Jolla.

Rostanga pulchra MacFarland, 1905. COLOR: The body is red with light markings and distinctively shaped rhinophores. RANGE: Vancouver Island, Canada, to Gulf of California; reported from Chile.

Tritonia festiva (Stearns, 1873). COLOR: It is pale orange with white markings. RANGE: Vancouver to Islas Los Coronados, Baja California Norte; Japan.

SEA HARE

Black Sea Hare

Common Sea Hare

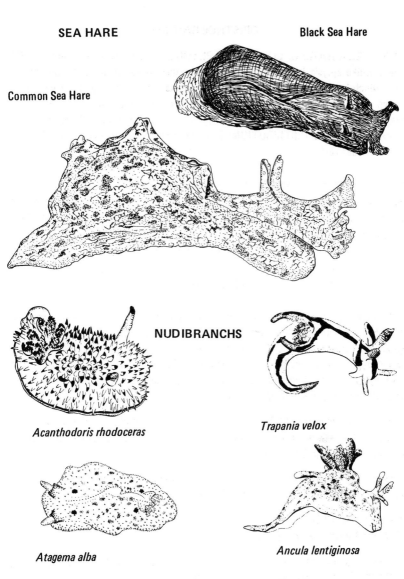

NUDIBRANCHS

Acanthodoris rhodoceras

Trapania velox

Atagema alba

Ancula lentiginosa

Rostanga pulchra

Tritonia festiva

75

NUDIBRANCHS

Cadlina flavomaculata MacFarland, 1905. COLOR: It is white with two brown rhinophores and 6-11 yellow spots on each side. RANGE: Canada to Baja California.

Melibe leonina (Gould, 1852). COLOR: They are pale yellow with white dots at the edge of the gills and on the hood. It catches small crustacean prey with the hood. RANGE: Alaska to the Gulf of California.

Hopkinsia rosacea MacFarland, 1905. COLOR: The body, head processes and gills are pink-red. The papillations are dark pink proximal and light pink distally. RANGE: Oregon to upper Baja California.

Triopha maculata MacFarland, 1905. COLOR: It is orange-brown with large white spots all over the body. The posterior placed gills are large. RANGE: Bodega Bay, California, to San Quintin, Baja California Norte.

Phidiana pugnax Lance, 1962. COLOR: Cerata on the back is dark and tipped with red. The body is white and the head with a red band anteriorly. Rhinophores or head processes cream distally with red beneath. The body is white. RANGE: Central California to Puerto Rompiente, Baja California Sur.

Hermissenda crassicornis (Eschscholtz, 1831). COLOR: An orange line is at the center of the head and the anterior part of the back. It is outlined with brilliant blue. The body is basically white. RANGE: Alaska to Gulf of California.

Chromodoris macfarlandi Cockerell, 1901. COLOR: It is brilliant reddish-violet with three bright yellow lines on the back. The edge of the back is white as is the edge of the foot. RANGE: Central California to central Baja California.

Hypselodoris californiensis (Bergh, 1879). COLOR: It is deep blue with large yellow dots or marks on the back, sides and top of tail. The edge of the back and foot is a lighter blue. RANGE: Central California to Bahía Magdalena, Baja California Sur. Also rarely seen in the Gulf of California.

The newly hatched nudibranchs and snail shells are called "veligers". The newly hatched clams and oysters are called "fry"; a bit larger they are called "spat". When clams are numerous on the bottom of the bay, they are called a bed of clams.

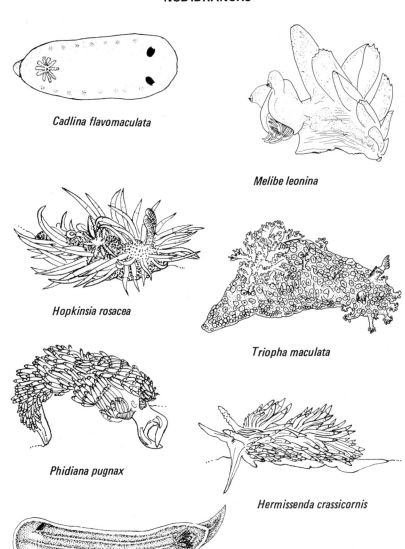

Cadlina flavomaculata

Melibe leonina

Hopkinsia rosacea

Triopha maculata

Phidiana pugnax

Hermissenda crassicornis

Chromodoris macfarlandi

Hypselodoris californiensis

77

NUDIBRANCHS

Aegires albopunctatus MacFarland, 1905. COLOR: White with black dots. RANGE: Vancouver Island, Washington, into Baja California and the Gulf of California.

Crimora coneja Marcus, 1961. COLOR: White with orange tipped dorsal processes. Some of the processes are bifurcated. RANGE: Cape Arago, Oregon, to Point Loma, California.

Dirona albolineata MacFarland in Cockerell & Eliot, 1905. COLOR: Translucent white with opaque white bands on cerata. RANGE: Puget Sound to San Diego.

Catriona columbiana (O'Donoghue, 1722). COLOR: Reddish cerata on a white body. RANGE: Puget Sound, Washington, to San Diego, California; Japan.

Polycera atra MacFarland, 1905. COLOR: Black and white with yellow markings. RANGE: Tomales Bay, California, to Baja California.

Flabellina iodinea (Cooper, 1863). COLOR: Purple with bright orange cerata and red rhinophores. RANGE: Vancouver Island, Canada, into Baja California, Mexico.

Dialulula sandiegensis (Cooper, 1862). COLOR: Pale yellow with dark rings and white gills. RANGE: Alaska to Gulf of California.

Janolus barbarensis (Cooper, 1863). COLOR: Translucent white body with bright blue and golden tipped cerata (dorsal processes). RANGE: British Columbia to northern Baja California.

Every one is interested in the treasures found in a tide pool at Casa Beach, La Jolla.

NUDIBRANCHS

Aegires albopunctatus

Crimora coneja

Dirona albolineata

Catriona columbiana

Polycera atra

Flabellina iodinea

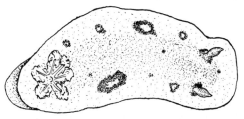

Diaulula sandiegensis

Janolus barbarensis

TUSK SHELL

HEXAGONAL TUSK SHELL, *Dentalium neohexagonum* Pilsbry & Sharp, 1897. This tusk shell is a slightly tapering and curved hexagon that attains a length of about two inches. It is white. RANGE: Monterey to Baja California and Gulf of California.

CEPHALOPODA

TWO-SPOTTED OCTOPUS or MUD-FLAT OCTOPUS, *Octopus bimaculoides* Pickford & MacConnaughey, 1949. Below its true eyes the two-spotted octopus has two false eyes, colored spots ringed with blue and darker than the rest of the body. It attains a diameter of about two feet. It lies in wait for passing fish or crab then darts out and captures it. Crabs seem to be its favorite food. The animal is usually some shade of brown; when disturbed, it may become warty and change color rapidly. RANGE: San Luis Obispo County, California, to Punta Baja, Baja California Norte. LOCAL DISTRIBUTION: Rocky intertidal areas.

OPALESCENT SQUID, *Loligo opalescens* Berry, 1911. The squid has ten sucker-bearing arms, one pair usually modified from the rest. The squid swims by use of fins, located near the tail and a siphon seen here between the eyes. It attains a length of ten inches. It is pale pink. RANGE: Puget Sound to Isla Quadalupe, Mexico. LOCAL DISTRIBUTION: Mission Bay and in deeper water off the coast. It is common.

At Cabrillo National Monument on Point Loma, seven persons beachcomb during a low tide. There is easy access from the parking lot down a slight cliff.

80

TUSK SHELL

Tusk Shell

CEPHALOPODS

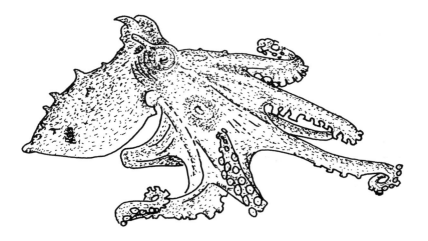

Two-Spotted Octopus

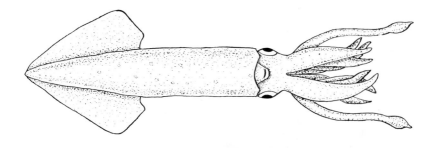

Opalescent Squid

BRACHIOPOD, *Laqueus californicus* (Koch, 1847). This lamp shell is attached to the substrate or to each other by means of a flexible peduncle. The shell is smooth with faint concentric lines. One valve is larger than the other; out of its base passes the flexible peduncle. The lamp shell is a pale orangish red. It attains a height of more than 2 inches. RANGE: Alaska to San Diego. LOCAL DISTRIBUTION: Deep water off our coast. It has been taken in water 40 and 75 fathoms.

BRACHIOPOD, *Glottidia albida* (Hinds, 1844). This brachiopod has a long peduncle which is used to pull itself down into its burrow at low tide or when disturbed. At other times the shell is half out of its retreat where currents bring food to it. The shell is laterally flattened. It is about an inch long and white. RANGE: Tomales Bay to Acapulco.

Four persons are enjoying the low tiding during a winter day at Bird Rock, La Jolla.

BRACHIOPOD

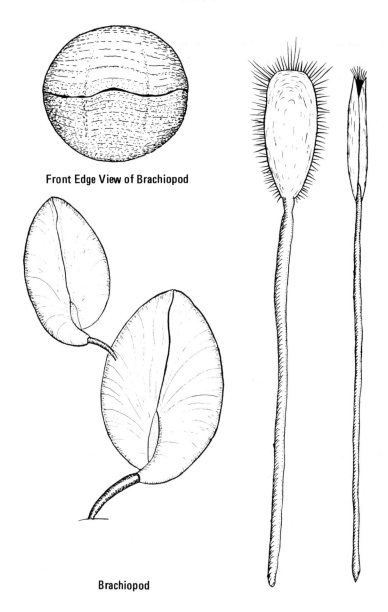

Front Edge View of Brachiopod

Brachiopod

Brachiopod

ECHINODERMS

Sea stars, sea urchins, sand dollars, and sea cucumbers are echinoderms. All are marine. They move or attach themselves by means of small but very numerous tube feet, each with a suction cup at the end. The echinoderms fall into five living classes.

Sea stars and sea urchins have many tiny pinchers (pedicellariae), which keep the animal free of homesteaders. If the sea star is held next to the back of your hand, the pedicellariae will pinch your hairs, and as the sea star is moved away, you will feel a pull on them.

SEA STARS - ASTEROIDEA

VARIABLE SEA STAR, *Linkia columbiae* Gray, 1840. This is a small sea star, sometimes five inches wide, which is highly variable as to form and number of arms; it is almost never symmetrical. Often the central disk bears only one or two arms. The arms are round and smooth, varying from a flat red, spotted with orange or yellow, to a flat tan with brighter specks. RANGE: San Pedro, California, to the Galapagos Islands. LOCAL DISTRIBUTION: Under rocks at low tide.

TWO-COLORED SEA STAR, *Pisaster giganteus* (Stimpson, 1857). This is similar to the ochre sea star but smaller, and attains a length of 15 inches. The knobby spines on the back are larger and do not form a pentagon on the central disk. One of the most distinctive characteristics of this animal is the color, usually an opalescent blue with the spines ringed with white. RANGE: Vancouver Island, British Columbia, to Ensendada, Baja California Norte. LOCAL DISTRIBUTION: Among rocks.

OCHRE SEA STAR, *Pisaster ochraceus* (Brandt, 1835). This is a large stiff-armed sea star densely covered with short rounded spines, which form a small pentagon on the central disk. It reaches a diameter of about five inches with smaller specimens being more common. The color varies from yellow to brown or red or purple. This is by far the most abundant sea star of southern California. RANGE: Alaska to Santa Barbara. There is a subspecies, *P. ochraceus segnis* Fisher, ranging to Ensenada, Baja California Norte. LOCAL DISTRIBUTION: Abundant on breakwaters, jetties, and piers, and occasionally under rocks.

SOFT SEA STAR, *Astrometis sertulifera* (Xantus, 1860). This animal is distinguished by the slender soft flexible arms, covered with many small spines. It may reach a diameter of seven inches. It is red-brown, with a faint tinge of blue-green around the base of the spines. RANGE: Santa Barbara, California, to the Gulf of California. LOCAL DISTRIBUTION: Under rocks.

SEA STARS

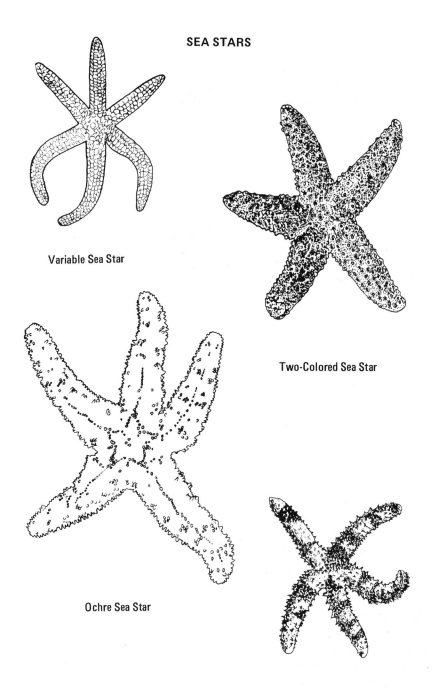

Variable Sea Star

Two-Colored Sea Star

Ochre Sea Star

Soft Sea Star

SEA STARS

BAT STAR or SEA BAT, *Patiria miniata* (Brandt, 1835). This sea star may be distinguished by its short webbed rays. It may reach a diameter of six inches, but a more typical size is one to two inches. The color varies from red to purple and orange to yellow, and may even be mixed. RANGE: Sitka, Alaska, to La Paz, Baja California Sur. LOCAL DISTRIBUTION: Abundant on jetties and around rocks; large individuals are often found in Mission Bay.

SAND SEA STAR, *Astropecten armatus* Gray, 1840. This sea star is purple-gray and rarely more than ten inches wide. A buried sand star can usually be located at low tide by a star-shaped disturbance in the sand. It eats various sand dwelling cnidarians, prosobranch and opisthobranch gastropods and echinoderms. RANGE: San Pedro, California, to Ecuador. LOCAL DISTRIBUTION: On sand flats in San Diego and Mission Bays.

A crowd admires a marlin and tuna catch at the Sport Fishing Docks on Point Loma.

SEA STARS

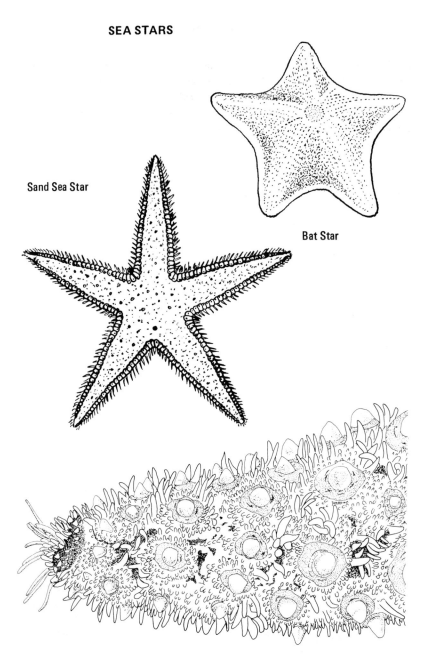

Sand Sea Star

Bat Star

Detail of an arm of a two-colored sea star. Note the blunt spines and elongated gills. The arm tip is light sensative.

SEA STARS

SUNFLOWER STAR, *Pycnopodia helianthoides* (Brandt, 1835). The sunflower star generally lives in shallow water further north and even intertidally. Here in San Diego it has been taken in deep water of about 100 feet where the water temperature rarely exceeds 60 degrees Fahrenheit. It has 20 or 24 rays in larger specimens and considerably fewer in young specimens. The sunflower star reaches a diameter of more than two feet. It has been reported in the past that specimens four feet in diameter may have occurred. It can be found in a variety of colors: bright red and purple, yellow and orange or gray. There are a few scattered white spines on the disk and rays. RANGE: Alaska to Bahía Totos Santos, Baja California Norte. LOCAL DISTRIBUTION: Deep water off our shore line.

LEATHER STAR, *Dermasterias imbricata* (Grube, 1857). This sea star has only recently been found in the San Diego area, its previous southern range being Monterey. It is light colored with red markings on the smooth skin. It smells like carbide and can be toxic in aquaria. It attains a size up to 10 inches. RANGE: Alaska to San Diego. LOCAL DISTRIBUTION: Mission Bay jetty.

SEA CUCUMBERS - HOLOTHUROIDEA

WHITE SEA CUCUMBER, *Leptosynapta albicans* (Selenka, 1867). This small sea cucumber is nearly translucent living buried in the sand. It is common but one must dig for it in order to find one. At first glace it might be mistaken for a worm. The animal is an off-white and lacks tube feet. It attains a length to six inches but two inch specimens are more common. RANGE: Puget Sound to San Diego. LOCAL DISTRIBUTION: It is reported to exist to depths of 600 feet. In the intertidal area it is found in the sandy or muddy substrate under rocks.

SWEET POTATO SEA CUCUMBER, *Caudina arenicola* (Stimpson, 1857). An unusual fact about this sea cucumber is that it has no tube feet or tentacles. The skin is tough, smooth and slippery. The animal lives buried in the sand and is occasionally found by digging one out. Pea crabs can usually be found in the digestive system. The sweet potato sea cucumber attains a length of nine inches. It is mottled yellow-brown. RANGE: Southern California and upper Baja California. LOCAL DISTRIBUTION: In Mission Bay at the low tide line.

SOUTHERN CALIFORNIA SEA CUCUMBER, *Parastichopus parvimensis* (Clark, 1913). The Southern California sea cucumber is a very soft cylindrical animal some 18 inches long, varying from yellow-brown to red-brown. The upper surface is covered with pointed warts, and the lighter underside bears tube feet. RANGE: Monterey Bay, California, to Punta Bartolome, Baja California Sur. LOCAL DISTRIBUTION: On the surface of sand and algae or under rocks and in tidepools.

SEA STARS

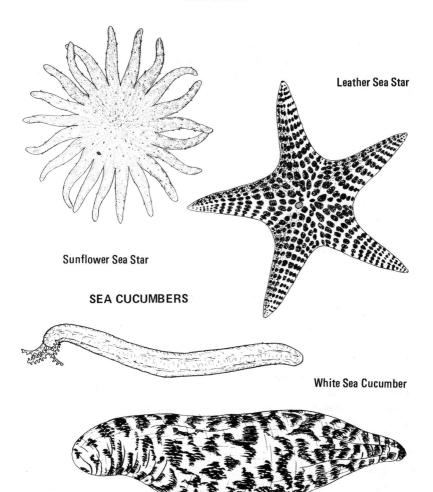

Leather Sea Star

Sunflower Sea Star

SEA CUCUMBERS

White Sea Cucumber

Sweet Potato Sea Cucumber

Southern California Sea Cucumber

BRITTLE STARS - OPHIOROIDEA

RINGED SERPENT BRITTLE STAR, *Ophionereis annulata* (La Conte, 1851). The ringed serpent star is brown and attains a diameter of four inches. The slender arms are ringed or spotted and have spines at acute angles. RANGE: San Pedro, California, to Equador and Galapagos Islands. LOCAL DISTRIBUTION: Under rocks along the coast.

SAND-COLORED BRITTLE STAR, *Ophioplocus esmarki* Lyman, 1874. This animal resembles the banded-armed brittle star but is smaller, reaching a diameter of only three and one-half inches with shorter arms only about three times the diameter of the central disk. The disk is covered with small swollen scales, which give it a pebbled appearance. It is a uniform light sandy-pink. RANGE: Tomales Bay (Marin County), California, to San Diego, California. LOCAL DISTRIBUTION: With other brittle stars under rocks.

BANDED-ARMED BRITTLE STAR, *Ophioderma panamense* Lütken 1859. The banded-armed brittle star is one of the most abundant and largest in this area, sometimes reaching a diameter of seven inches. It is dark brown with alternating light and dark bands encircling the arms. The solid-colored disk is finely granulated with a notch over each arm. RANGE: San Pedro, California, to Panama, Galapagos Islands and Peru (five degrees south). LOCAL DISTRIBUTION: Abundant under rocks.

BLUNT-SPINED BRITTLE STAR, *Ophiopteris papillosa* (Lyman, 1875). The blunt-spined brittle star may reach a diameter of seven inches. It is brown with numerous darker bands encircling the arms. Each arm bears five rows of close-set, erect, small, square-cut spines. RANGE: Vancouver Island, British Columbia, to Isla Cedros, Baja California. LOCAL DISTRIBUTION: Under rocks.

SPINY BRITTLE STAR, *Ophiothrix spiculata* La Conte, 1851. The arms of the spiny brittle star are covered with spines that are longer, thinner, and more numerous than those of the blunt-spined brittle star. The central disk is so thickly covered with small spines that it often appears fuzzy. It attains a diameter of seven inches. The color is highly variable but often is green-brown. RANGE: San Mateo County, California, to Central America, Galapagos Islands and Peru. LOCAL DISTRIBUTION: Under rocks.

The shape of sea urchins range from flat to round. Some sand dollars are flat, and those known as sea biscuits are a semi-round form. The most common sea urchins have a round form. The former have very short spines; the latter very long spines. The beaches usually have sand dollars of only the skeleton or "test" with no spines.

BRITTLE STARS

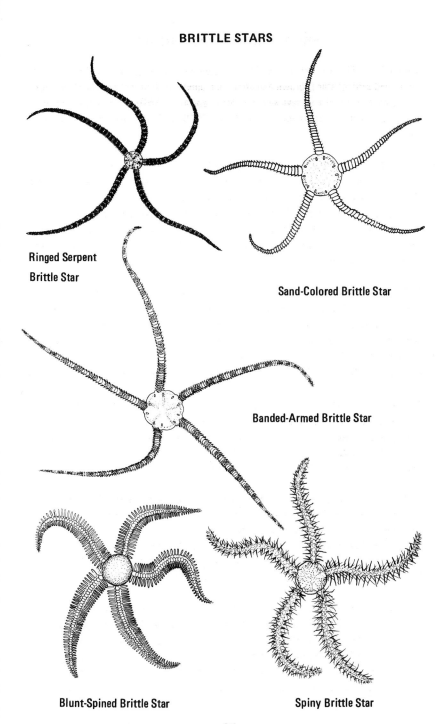

Ringed Serpent
Brittle Star

Sand-Colored Brittle Star

Banded-Armed Brittle Star

Blunt-Spined Brittle Star

Spiny Brittle Star

SEA URCHINS - ECHINOIDEA

PURPLE SEA URCHIN, *Strongylocentrotus purpuratus* (Stimpson, 1857). The purple sea urchin is covered with short, blunt, movable spines. It may reach a diameter of two inches. The color varies from green in the young to a deep purple in the adults. RANGE: British Columbia, Canada, to Isla Cedros, Baja California Norte. LOCAL DISTRIBUTION: Common locally on rock ledges and jetties and under rocks.

PALE SEA URCHIN, *Lytechinus anamesus* H. L. Clark, 1912. The pale sea urchin resembles a purple sea urchin in shape except for shorter spines. The color is a greyish white. It is somewhat smaller and attains a diameter of about one and one-half inches. It is often in large herds. RANGE: Channel Islands into the Gulf of California. LOCAL DISTRIBUTION: In the San Diego river flood control channel about the eel grass and at times in the upper part of the plant.

BANDED SPINED SEA URCHIN, *Centrostephanus coronatus* (Verrill, 1867). The spines are typically slender and very long dorsally, not so long laterally. The spines have up to eight narrow dark bands. It can reach a diameter of two and one-half inches and a height of five inches. The animal generally appears as a deep purple-red. RANGE: Southern California to the Galapagos Islands. LOCAL DISTRIBUTION: Extremely low tide line to over 300 feet depth.

RED SEA URCHIN, *Strongylocentrotus franciscanus* (A. Agassiz, 1863). The largest urchin in these waters attains a "test" diameter of up to 100 mm. It is not as abundant intertidally as the purple sea urchin. RANGE: Alaska to Isla Cedros, Baja California Norte. LOCAL DISTRIBUTION: About large rocks and subtidally.

The spine of the heart urchin and other urchins and sand dollars fit onto a ball on the test of the animal. At the base of the spine is a socket to fit onto the ball. The spine is directed toward a stimulation or predatory fish by muscles at the base of the spine. On a purple sea urchin still in place in the sea water, one spine can be gently touched and several spines next to it will move toward the spine you stimulated by touch. The urchin is trying not to be a meal. The sand dollar has very small spines. The sand dollar will half bury in the sand and lean into the current. The sand dollar is allowing the currents to bring food items to it .

SEA URCHINS

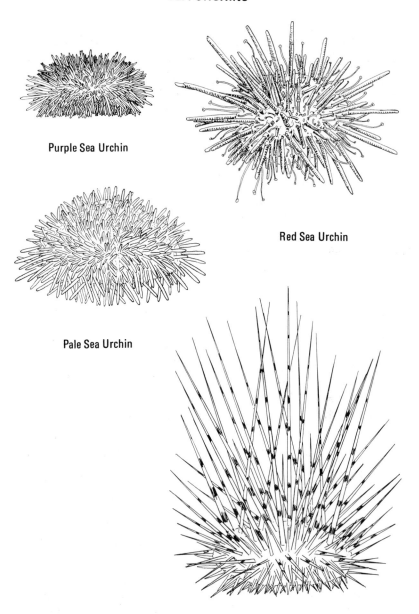

Purple Sea Urchin

Red Sea Urchin

Pale Sea Urchin

Banded Spined Sea Urchin

SEA URCHINS - ECHINOIDEA

SAND DOLLAR, *Dendraster excentricus* (Eschscholtz, 1831). The sand dollar is a flattened sea urchin and reaches a diameter of three inches. Close examination will reveal tiny spines corresponding to those of a sea urchin, though these are missing from the dead shell or "test" often found on the beach. RANGE: Alaska to central Baja California. LOCAL DISTRIBUTION: Found in the flood control channel of the San Diego River, Mission Bay and La Jolla Shores.

HEART URCHIN, *Lovenia cordiformis* (A. Agassiz, 1872). The heart urchin can on rare occasions be found moving across the surface of the sand. It generally lies buried in the sand below the low tide line and more commonly in very deep water. Characteristic are the extremely long aboral spines on the interambulacral region. It is white. The heart urchin attains a length of about two inches. RANGE: San Pedro to Panama. LOCAL DISTRIBUTION: A specimen was found on the surface of the sand on Tierra Del Fuego in Mission Bay. It is sometimes common in the shallow subtidal at La Jolla Shores. Primarily found in deep water off the coast. See color print at front of book.

CRINOID

SEA LILIES or CRINOIDS. Many of the crinoids have cirri, as shown in the drawing. It is used to hold the animal to the substrate temporarily. This animal has five arms which branch at their base for a total of ten feather-like rays. This animal attains a length of about three and one-half inches. Preserved animals are warm tan. RANGE: Mostly warm seas. LOCAL DISTRIBUTION: The crinoid drawn here came from the 30 mile bank west of Point Loma in 1,241 feet or 378 meters of water.

Inside the test or shell of a sea urchin is an elaborate apparatus called the Aristotle's lantern, for it suggests a lantern of yesteryear. It has five parts with a tooth at the end of each. These teeth and apparatus are used to feed with and are of local concern because with these five teeth vast amounts of algae are eaten, including some of the more beneficial algas to mankind. Sea urchins have been controlled to some extent to prevent this devastation. In some societies some parts of the insides of sea urchins are considered a delectable food item and sometimes eaten on soda crackers.

CRINOID

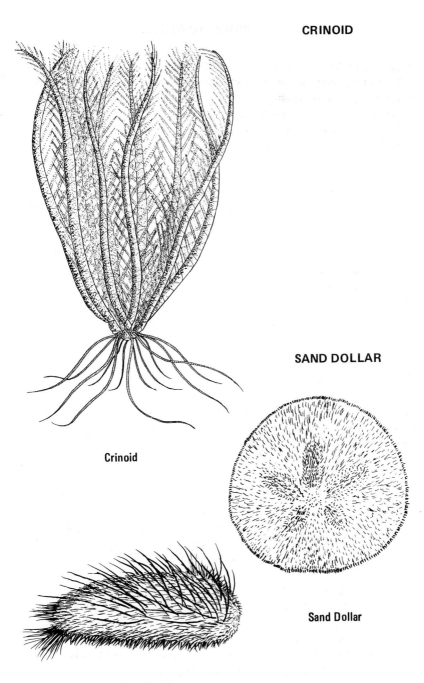

Crinoid

SAND DOLLAR

Sand Dollar

Heart Urchin

95

CHORDATE

The chordate is the major group that includes the vertebrate animals — fish, amphibians, reptiles, birds, and mammals — all of which have backbones. The chordates also include three small groups of marine animals without backbones but with other striking points of resemblance to the vertebrates.

The adult tunicate (a non-vertebrate chordate) is sedentary, either solitary or forming colonies that might be taken for sponges. But the free-swimming tadpole-like young have gill slits and in other ways resemble fish. Tunicates are so called because of their tough outer "tunic," of a cellulose-like material.

Though most larger fish retreat with the ebbing tide, some small ones survive the low tides in tide pools, where a little bit of high water is trapped. They hide under rocks and seaweed.

TUNICATES

STALKED SIMPLE TUNICATE, *Stylea montereyensis* (Dall, 1872). The stalked simple tunicate is leathery brown and about eight inches long. RANGE: British Columbia to Isla San Geronimo, Baja California. LOCAL DISTRIBUTION; On the floats of docks and on pilings in bays.

SIMPLE TUNICATE, *Ciona intestinalis* (Linnaeus, 1767). The simple tunicate grows in great clusters in the spring and summer on the floats and docks in bays. It reaches a length of about three inches. It is green-yellow with the internal anatomy showing through the thin body wall. RANGE: Alaska to San Diego. LOCAL DISTRIBUTION: On pilings, flats, and docks in Mission and San Diego Bays.

FISH - PISCES

HORN SHARK, *Heterodontus francisci* (Girard, 1854). This five gill slit shark has two dorsal fins with a spine in front. The shark grows to four feet. The color is pale brown with scattered dark spots. RANGE: Monterey Bay, California, to the Gulf of California. LOCAL DISTRIBUTION: Common in shallow water, rare in the intertidal areas.

CALIFORNIA MORAY EEL, *Gymnothorax mordax* (Ayres, 1859). The moray eel has very sharp teeth and a medial tooth in the palate behind the other upper jaw jeeth. It reaches five feet long, but usually less than three footers are seen in the tide pools. It is dark brown with yellow or green markings. It generally feeds on octopus and fish. Range: Point Conception, California, to Bahía Magdalena, Baja California Sur. LOCAL DISTRIBUTION: Rocky intertidal pools and subtidal areas.

TUNICATE

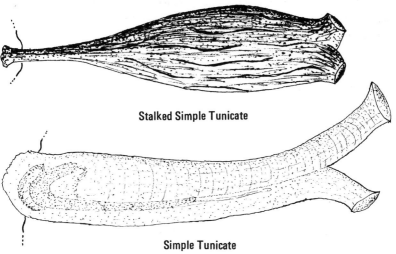

Stalked Simple Tunicate

Simple Tunicate

FISH

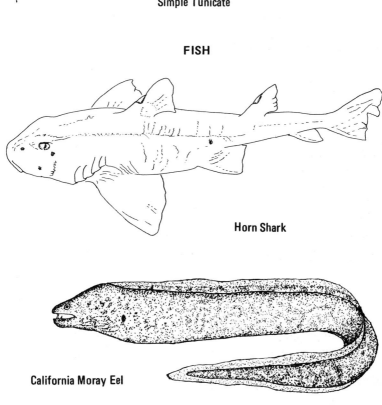

Horn Shark

California Moray Eel

FISH - PISCES

BLIND GOBY, *Typhlogobius californiensis* Steindachner, 1880. The blind goby is uniformly pink and has no scales. It grows to a length of two and one-half inches. When young, it has two black dots in the usual location of the eyes. Within six months the cornea becomes twisted and overgrown by flesh, making the eye non-functional. RANGE: San Simeon Point, California, to Bahía Magdalena, Baja California Sur. LOCAL DISTRIBUTION: Fairly abundant at Bird Rock, La Jolla, though seldom seen because it lives under the surface. One or two blind gobies may be found in the burrow of a ghost shrimp.

WOOLY SCULPIN, *Clinocottus analis* (Girard, 1858). The wooly sculpin is often seen on the bottom of a tide pool moving about in a jerky manner. It attains a length of seven inches, although small specimens about three inches long are more common. Its color changes to match its background, but commonly it is mottled, pale green or black, and spotted with white dots. RANGE: Cape Mendocino, California, to Punta Ascuncion, Baja California Sur. LOCAL DISTRIBUTION: In tide pools.

SPOTTED KELPFISH, *Gibbonsia elegans* (Cooper, 1864). When a tide pool is approached, its occupants generally hide in the algae or under rocks. If you wait quietly for a while, the spotted kelpfish, which blends well into the background, will begin to move about and can be detected. The spotted kelpfish, about four inches long, is brown with two prominent blue or brown spots on each side of the tail and above the pectoral fin. RANGE: Point Piedras Blancas, California, to Bahía Magdalena, Baja California Sur. LOCAL DISTRIBUTION: In tide pools at very low tide.

CALIFORNIA CLINGFISH, *Gobiesox rhessodon* Smith, 1811. The clingfish is a flattened fish about two inches long with characteristically U-shaped pelvic fins with which it adheres to rocks. It is light brown. It is seldom seen because of its size, its protective color, and its ability to hide. RANGE: Santa Cruz Island and Gaviota, California, to Isla Guadalupe and Bahía San Bartolome, Baja California Sur. LOCAL DISTRIBUTION: Under rocks at low tide.

Some fish-scale types found on fish in these waters are:

1. PLACOID SCALES or plate-like as found on sharks and rays.
2. CYCLOID SCALES as with salmon-like fish and soft-rayed fined species.
3. CTENOID SCALES have on them a posterior margin that is comblike. Fish with spines as well as soft rays in their fins usually have this kind of scale; i.e, the sea basses.

FISH

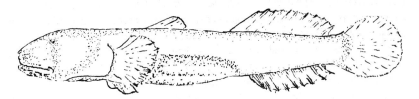

Blind Goby

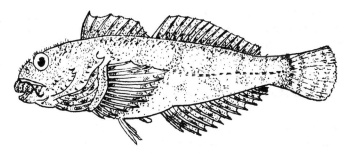

Wooly Sculpin

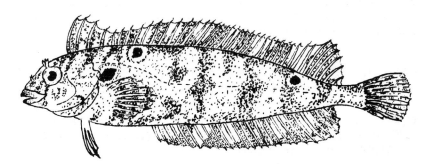

Spotted Kelpfish

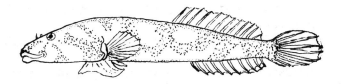

California Cling Fish

FISH - PISCES

OPALEYE, *Girella nigricans* (Ayres, 1860). The opaleye can be distinguished in the tidepools by the white blotch on each side of its back, contrasting with its light to dark green overall color. It has eyes of an opalescent blue. It attains a length of 15 inches, but small ones about three or four inches are the rule in tide pools. The opaleye feeds on seaweed covered with animal life, such as bryozoans and hydroids. RANGE: San Francisco, California, to Cabo San Lucas, Baja California Sur. LOCAL DISTRIBUTION: In rocky areas and in the highest tide pools.

PACIFIC SEAHORSE, *Hippocampus ingens* Girard, 1858. This fish is golden yellow with white spotting. The male raises the young in a brood pouch. The tail is prehensile. It attains a length of 12 inches. RANGE: San Diego to Peru. LOCAL DISTRIBUTION: Very rare, most likely about algae. Several were collected in 1985 and 1986.

GARIBALDI, *Hypsypops rubicundus* (Girard, 1854). The young are orange with bright blue blotches and spots. Adults are a uniform bright golden-orange similar to the brilliantly colored shirts worn by the troops of Garibaldi in Italy during the mid 1800's. It attains a length of 14 inches. RANGE: Monterey Bay, California, to Bahía Magdalena, Baja California Sur. LOCAL DISTRIBUTION: The young are seen at low, low tide in rocky tidepools. The species is protected by law.

SHINER SURFPERCH, *Cymatogaster aggregata* Gibbons, 1854. This active fish is "secretive". It is silvery when seen from the side and gray above. There are three yellow bars on the side. This fish attains a size of seven inches but those in tidepools are much smaller. It bears live young from eggs hatched within. This is known as being viviparous. RANGE: Port Wrangell, Alaska, to Bahía San Quintin, Baja California Norte. LOCAL DISTRIBUTION: Seen in rocky tidepools.

CALIFORNIA GRUNION, *Leuresthes tenuis* (Ayres, 1860). During the full and new moons grunion runs may fill the beaches of southern California. Times for spawning are during the months of March through August with April and May, the peak of the spawning period, closed to fishing. The eggs are buried in the sand then fertilized by the male. Two weeks later the eggs are ready to hatch and are washed out of their resting place. RANGE: San Francisco to Bahía Magdalena, Baja California Sur. LOCAL DISTRIBUTION: Rare for those anglers who try to run and do not see any fish. Otherwise on sandy beaches with good surf on the peak high tides every two weeks. Consult a tide table or local newspaper for expected times for the grunion runs.

The northern anchovy feeds upon phytoplankton and zooplankton and is a filter feeder. The basking shark is a filter feeder also, sifting with gill rakers and growing up to 15 to 45 feet.

FISH

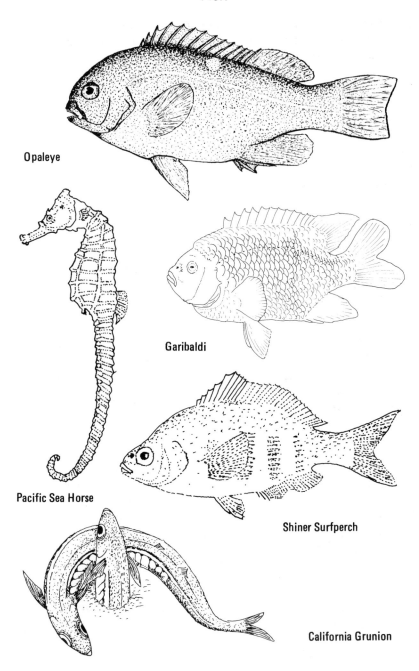

Opaleye

Garibaldi

Pacific Sea Horse

Shiner Surfperch

California Grunion

BIRDS - AVES

BRANDT'S CORMORANT, *Phalacrocrax penicillatus* Brant, 1837. It has a light band across the throat. The rest of the plumage is a deep brown, appearing black from a distance. The tip of the bill is hooked and sharp. The bird is about three feet high, standing. They are seen sunning on beach rocks. They may hold the wings outstretched to dry their feathers that become wet from diving for fish or crustaceans. RANGE: Southern Canada to Baja California. LOCAL DISTRIBUTION: At sea, flying in formation along the coast, littoral or even on inland bodies of water.

BROWN PELICAN, *Pelecanus occidentalis* Linnaeus, 1766. A wing spread to six and one-half feet is outstretched as the bird skims over the water's surface. It flies in formation or by itself. When feeding, it will dive into the water holding its extended wings back plunging into the water with its mouth open. The under part of the bill expanded with water and fish, the bird allows the water to filter out. It then swallows the fish. RANGE: On this coast from southern U. S. to South America. LOCAL DISTRIBUTION: At sea, bays, rocks along the coast and inland bodies of water also.

AMERICAN GOLDEN PLOVER, *Pluvialis dominica* Muller, 1776. A migrant bird seen at a rocky beach is here illustrated in nonbreeding plumage. A white band extends over the eyes. The back is brown and mottled. The legs are gray. It grows to about ten inches. RANGE: Arctic America, Hawaii, South America and many other localities. Sparse in California. LOCAL DISTRIBUTION: Mudflats and shores.

HERRING GULL, *Larus argentatus,* Pontoppidan, 1763. The adult gull has white spots or "mirrors" within the black at the tips of the primary flight feathers. The bird has a red spot at the end of the lower bill. It has flesh colored legs. It is about 25 inches tall. RANGE: Northern hemesphere. LOCAL DISTRIBUTION: At sea, along the coast, bays, beaches and also inland.

MAMMALS - MAMMALIA

CALIFORNIA SEA LION, *Zalophus californianus* (Lessom, 1828). Readily identified from the external ears. The sea lion has whiskers on its chin and hair covering its body. The flippers are analogous to our hands containing bone for bone. These agile swimmers, are carnivores, feeding on fish and squid. RANGE: North America and Baja California. LOCAL DISTRIBUTION: Ocean, off shore islands and coastal areas and bays. They can readily be seen around fishing piers.

GRAY WHALE, *Eschrichtius robustus* (Lilljeborg, 1861). The adult leviathan attains a length of 45 feet and may be 20 tons. It migrates south within a mile or so along the Pacific coast of North America to calve and mate in lagoons and bays of Baja California and Mexico. This is done in the winter months primarily. Whale watching boats may be boarded for a couple hours to get a closer view of them. RANGE: Bering Sea to Mexico. LOCAL DISTRIBUTION: A mile off shore heading south and further out to sea on northward migration. On occasion one may wash ashore.

BIRDS

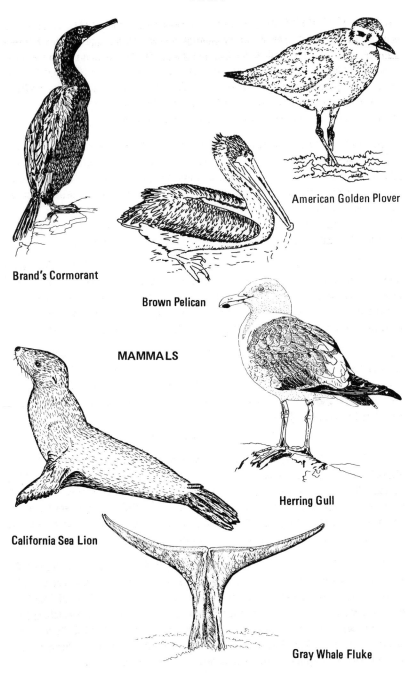

Brand's Cormorant

Brown Pelican

American Golden Plover

MAMMALS

Herring Gull

California Sea Lion

Gray Whale Fluke

103

CONSERVATION

1. A ROCKY BEACH NATURE WALK

Perhaps you might like to experience a typical outing to the tide pools of Bird Rock, La Jolla, California. Here the intertidal scene is a gentle slope where a large rocky littoral is exposed at ebb tides. There are two or three good ebb tides appearing on a Saturday afternoon that will be good for an outing. They occur some time between October and March. The local newspaper (or tide calendar) is consulted for tide predictions for this area.

The time for the trip arrives. If it is a cool, cloudy, wintery day, perhaps ten people will be present for the experience. But if it is a warm sunny day, perhaps a hundred people will be present to hear and explore sea life in the area. There will be young and old alike to take part in the venture.

Today, as the group looks out over the tide flats, one can see some of the 200 people here bending over looking for sea shells, sea stars, crabs, or some other marine creature. Some of my tidepoolers are early arrivers and begin trickling over to the starting point. Others, out of curiosity and seeing a crowd on the beach, come over to see what it is all about and join in the adventure. This day we will have a small group.

The time is 1:40, five minutes before the trip was announced to start and an hour before the tide is to change and come back in. The hand-out sheets listing the common marine animals in the area are ready to be handed out. It is now 1:45 and the people begin gathering around.

An example of the 80-some common animals listed on the hand-out sheets is as follows:

ECHINODERMATA (SEA STARS, SEA URCHINS, BRITTLE STARS, SEA CUCUMBERS, ETC.)

1. Soft Sea Star   *Astrometis sertulifera*
2. Ochre Sea Star   *Piaster ochraceus*
3. Two-colored Sea Star   *Piaster giganteus*
4. Variable Sea Star   *Linkia columbiae*
5. Sea Bat Sea Star   *Patiria miniata*
6. Southern California Sea Cucumber   *Parastichopus parvimensis*
7. Purple Sea Urchin   *Strongylocentrotus purpuratus*

I give the scientific name with the common name because it is specific. As an example, consider the bat sea star; it is also known as webbed sea star and broad armed sea star. The question arises: which is correct? They are all correct for different areas, but *Patiria miniata* (page 86) is the scientific name and the only one it has.

The hand-out sheets are distributed and the trip across the rocky intertidal area is ready to begin. In the way of an introduction, speaking over the surf pounding in the distance, it is explained that San Diego is fortunate to have this fine rocky intertidal beach, even though many of the animals fall prey to the collectors' hands and end up in a bucket. The area gives up many secrets over the hour or two a collector may be looking for sea life.

There are a few other choice intertidal areas about the county where people might go to see sea life. One is at the foot of Hill Street on Point Loma and the other area is a Marine Biological Preserve near the Scripps Institution of Oceanography. Here no collecting is permitted.

It is explained that the animals should be left for others to enjoy, for if the 200-some people on the beach were to take home two animals each, 400 animals would have been removed from the beach, and tomorrow a few more, and next month a few more, and so on. This is only half the problem; for when a rock is turned over to see what lurks beneath, and is not replaced, the animals needing the protection from exposure will die and the algae will die for lack of sunlight. In this case many more animals are "removed" from the areas. So it is recommended that a rock that has been looked under be replaced.

There are four zones where the animals live in the littoral and all are covered in the trek across the rocky shore. There is the SPLASH ZONE on the face of the cliff at Bird Rock where one will find two kinds of periwinkle shells: *Littorina* (page 60), and the rock louse, *Ligia* (page 20). In the HIGH TIDE ZONE can be found the black turban shell, *Tegula* (page 56), and the striped shore crab, *Pachygrapsus* (page 36). The MIDDLE TIDE ZONE harbors the conspicuous chiton, *Stenoplax* (page 70), and the soft sea star, *Astrometis* (page 84). In the LOW TIDE ZONE the southern California sea cucumber, *Parastichopus* (Page 88) and the kelp crab, *Pugettia* (page 34), may be found.

We progress across the rocks, finding animals along the way. The children on the trip participate by looking for their own animals, as Bill and Leslie have done in finding a sea star, and bring them up for identification. Most of the children bring plastic bags, small buckets, or jars for their new-found treasures. They either take them to school to share the sea creatures with the other children or start a collection or a marine aquarium. Children collect more sea-things than adults. They are brave, delving into the unknown, not fearful of what they might find.

The sea stars are covered with very small beak-like pinchers called pedicellaria that clamp onto the hair on the back of the hand or arm when brought into contact. They tug at the hair but do not cause any harm. The sharp spines of the sea urchin (page 92) can become embedded in a careless collector's finger. Once in a great while an octopus (page 4 and 80) might bite with its parrot-like beak, or if it does not bite, may squirt water and black ink all over your clothes; this happened to me. A finger may be cut on a sharp edge of the scaled worm shell, *Serpulorbis* (page 64), found on the under sides of the rocks in the middle tide zone, just at that crucial place where one might put his hands when turning over a rock. Such a cut might fester for a few days if not treated. A good idea is to have a bandage in your pocket just in case. If a sea hare is handled too roughly it might secrete a purple fluid on the hands, causing some staining. Another animal that might bite is the moray eel (page 96) found in the low tide zone. Usually it is more frightened than the collector and scurries off to deeper parts.

Some of the animals found in the intertidal area are very conspicuous, like the colorful sea slugs or nudibranchs (pages 74-79) and the sea hare (page 74). The sea hare at times is left high and damp on the surface of the rocks where it is very conspicuous and easily captured. Here it waits for the incoming tide so that it might begin feeding on the brown and red algae. There are two kinds of sea hares: one called the common sea hare, *Aplysia californica* (page 74), which has a pointed tail, and the other cow-like aplysia, *Aplysia vaccaria* (page 74), so named because of its cow-like grazing habits. It has a rounded tail. Other animals blend into the background of the tide pools so that one could look directly at the animal and not realize it was there. This is true of some of the tide pool fish, such as the sculpins (page 96) and kelpfish (page 88).

We begin making our way across the beach and stop at a likely spot to dig under the rocks. A beach ghost shrimp, *Callianassa affinis* (page 28) and the blind goby *Typhlogobius californiensis* (page 99) are found; they live together in a tunnel in the wet sand. They are fairly common and can generally be found where there is an indication of ghost shrimp—look for a small (about ¼ inch) hole in the sand under rocks. The beach ghost shrimp may be 2½ inches long and is generally whitish or cream in color. One claw is greatly enlarged. The blind goby is a fish about 2½ inches long, uniformly pink, and without scales. One or two blind gobies may be found in the burrow of a ghost shrimp. When young, the blind goby has two black dots in the usual location of the eyes. Within six months the corneas become twisted and overgrown by flesh, making the eyes nonfunctional. These animals are quite common at Bird Rock in the middle tide zone, though seldom seen, as they live under the surface.

Bob, in a rush of excitement, brings me a giant keyhole limpet, *Megathura crenulata* (page 51). I explain that it is massive, sometimes seven inches long. The foot of the animal is orange-yellow, almost the color of a cantaloupe. There is a black or tan mantle which nearly covers the shell. Sometimes located between the sides of the foot and the mantle is a dark commensal shrimp.

Audrey brings a southern California sea cucumber, *Parastichopus parvimensis* (page 88), for the group to see. It is a very soft cylindrical animal some eighteen inches long in the water. Out of the water it is shorter and somewhat tense and firm. It varies in color from yellow-brown to red-brown. The upper surface is covered with pointed warts, and the lighter underside bears tube feet similar to starfish and other spiny-skinned animals. Sometimes one can find a pea crab, *Pinnixa* (Page 38), living in the cloaca of the sea cucumber. The pea crab is not harming the sea cucumber, but the sea cucumber is providing a home for the pea crab.

Ross hands me a masking crab, *Loxorhynchus crispatus* (page 36). I point out that it is a walking garden of seaweeds and loses all resemblance to a crab. The crab glues the seaweeds on its legs and back until it has virtually blended well into its home grounds. The crab reaches a length of about 4½ inches.

A tide pool reveals a navanax, *Navanax inermis* (page 4 and 40). It is a sea hare about four inches long, with many yellow dots and stripes and a few blue dots on a brown background. When disturbed, the navanax extrudes a yellow fluid smoke screen to discourage intruders. The ones living along the coast are smaller than the ones which live in bays and are about seven inches long, probably because more food is available there. Navanax eat their relatives, the nudibranchs and bubble shells. Navanax will home in on the trail of a nudibranch or bubble shell, and like a vacuum cleaner swallow down its prey in one swift gulp. At times the bubble shell can be felt inside the navanax. After the soft parts are digested the shell is expelled. Since the nudibranch has no shell, the only hard parts left are its teeth.

We have looked for and found many marine animals during the past two hours. As many as 57 different animals have been found. Some of the animals we have discovered include sea anemones with their sides covered with bits of shells and sand. We have brought up several kinds of orange, white, and olive colored flatworms (page 14), seen scurrying for darker parts when the rock was looked under. We have found peanut worms (page 16), so called because when retracted they resemble a peanut kernel. Also seen were three kinds of sea stars, several brittlestars, a sea cucumber, and many purple sea urchins. The group saw three kinds of barnacles, a shrimp, hermit crabs, porcelain or flat-topped crabs, and the common striped shore crab. About 25 different kinds of mollusks were seen, including the sea hare, giant keyhole limpet, abalone, wavy top shell, conspicuous chiton, and two-spotted octopus. We also saw solitary tunicates or sea squirts, and in the way of fish, the tide-pool sculpin, cling fish, tide-pool blenny, opaleye, and the blind goby.

The guided walk has come to an end but may of the people remain in the area to find more animals for themselves and to see if they can find an octopus, sea star, sea hare, or some other marine animal; the tide will be out for a few more minutes.

A teacher writes to me after the outing that he took a poll of this class prior to the trip and found that only one of his 25 students had been to the rocky tide pools. He remedied that by taking them on my trip and wrote that, "The children were as happy as if it were Christmas morning. They climbed all over the rocks, picking up everything in sight, but were careful to turn the rocks back over. They also returned all the specimens to the ocean except a few which we selected for our tide pool loaner aquarium. The loaner aquarium is circulated among the homes of the children to give them a chance to observe the living habits of the specimens in their own home after school hours and to write about their first-hand observations."

Do you have a rocky or sandy intertidal area nearby? Take some time to observe and discover the sea shore life. But please, turn that rock back over!

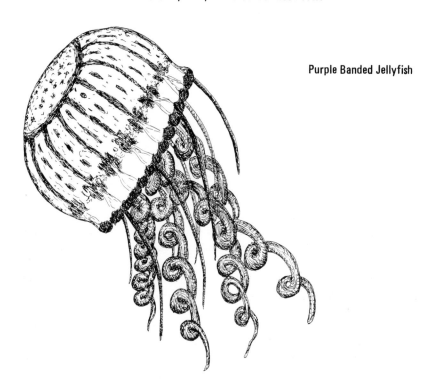

Purple Banded Jellyfish

PURPLE BANDED JELLYFISH, *Pelagia colorata* Russell, 1964. It has a bell diameter of up to 40 inches. It washes ashore occasionally. The stinging nematocysts cause a fierce reaction. RANGE: The west coast of the United States.

CONSERVATION

2. THE BIRD ROCK CENSUS

Data from October to March 1957 of the Bird Rock Census was tabulated by Wesley M. Farmer and Jack L. Littlepage. The time spent collecting data was 97.5 hours. The number of people that had not collected anything was 798. People that had collected some sea life was 1,140. The number of preschool youngsters was 54, grammer school children 284, Junior high school children 251, high school children 210, and 49 middle aged people. The population of the people collecting was: 728 first timers; 100 second timers; 179 occasional visitors; 318 frequent visitors. The question was asked, "Do you have a sea life collection?" There were 204 "yes" answers and 543 "no's."

The list of species collected are given with the number of specimens collected or taken from the area arranged by how many were taken. They are:

WESTERN BANDED TEGULA, *Tegula eiseni* 868
CONSPICUOUS CHITON, *Stenoplax conspicua* 581
BLACK TEGULA, *Tegula funebralis*. 568
various LIMPETS, i.e. *Collisella, Lottis*. 457
GREEN ABALONE, *Haliotis fulgens*. 376
PERIWINKLES, *Littorina spp.* 318
CALIFORNIA COMMON SEA HARE, *Aplysia californica* 301
LINED SHORE CRAB, *Pachygrapsus crassipes* 298
SPINY BRITTLE STAR, *Ophiothrix spiculata* 246
HERMIT CRABS, *Pagurus spp.*. 226
RINGED SERPENT BRITTLE STAR, *Ophionereis annulata* 150
TWO SPOTTED OCTOPUS, *Octopus bimaculoides* 147
BAT STAR, *Patiria miniata* 141
SOFT SEA STAR, *Astrometis sertulifera* 131
GIANT GREEN SEA ANEMONE, *Anthopleura xanthogrammica* 129
WAVY TURBAN, *Astraea undosa* 126
BANDED—ARMED BRITTLE STAR, *Ophioderma panamense* 110
SAND—COLORED BRITTLE STAR, *Ophioplocus esmarki*. 107
various FLATWORM species 98
VOLCANO LIMPET, *Fissurella volcano* 82
PURPLE SEA URCHIN, *Strongylocentrotus purpuratus* 74
COMMON ROCK CRAB, *Cancer antennarius*. 53
NAVANAX, *Navanax inermis*. 51

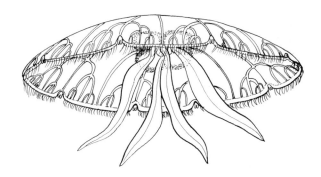

Moon Jellyfish

MOON JELLYFISH,   *Aurelia aurita* (Linnaeus, 1758). It grows to 16 inches wide. It stings from   tentacles under the bell producing a slight rash from mild toxins. RANGE: Alaska to southern California, world wide.

111

BIRD ROCK CENSUS

	OCT.	NOV.	DEC.	JAN.	FEB.	MAR.	Totals
Total People	344	707	700	136	433	332	2,652
People Checked	130	448	567	122	382	291	1,940
People Passed by	214	259	133	14	51	41	712
% With Collection	66%	78%	64%	30%	53%	37%	55%
% Without Collection	34%	22%	36%	70%	47%	63%	45%
People Checked With Collection	86	349	360	37	203	107	1,142
Total Animals Observed	227	552	448	42	230	122	1,621
Number Animals Taken Calculated	474	2,627	2,193	117	642	714	6,767
Man Hours Collecting	1,246	4,170	2,720	133	725	813	9,807
Calculated Man Hours	109	529	541	110	400	393	2,082
Animals Per Man Hour	288	974	668	450	450	2,953	2,953
Animals Per Person	4.34	4.98	4.05	1.61	1.81	3.0	3.0
Total People With Animals	5.5	7.55	6.10	3.16	6.66	3.35	3.35

The total of the collection tabulated from 1,940 people checked was 6,767 animals. We counted 712 people that hurried by and so could not check their collections. By calculations it is found that 9,807 animals were taken during the total calculated man hours (2,953 hunting hours) spent looking in the intertidal area for sea life.

3. PHYLA OF LIVING ORGANISMS, PLANTS and ANIMALS
(Monerans, Protistans, Plants and Animals)

PHYLA	SPECIES	NAME	HABITAT

MONERANS	MONERANS	MONERANS	MONERANS	MONERANS

1. Schizophyta . . . . (2,00)   Bacteria . . . . PTMF
2. Xyanophyta . . . . (2,500)   Blue-green Algae . . . . TMF

PROTISTANS	PROTISTANS	PROTISTANS	PROTISTANS	PROTISTANS

1. Matigophora . . . . ( )   Flagellates . . . . PMF
2. Rhizopoda . . . . ( )   Amoebas . . . . PMF
3. Sporazoa . . . . ( )   Plasmodium . . . . P
4. Ciliophora . . . . (6,000)   Ciliates, *Paramecium* . . . . .MF
5. Myxomycetes . . . . ( )   Slime Molds . . . . T
6. Mycophyta . . . . . . (57,000)   Fungi-yeasts, Mushrooms . . . . . . T
7. Chlorophyta . . . . (6,750)   Green Algae . . . . TMF
8. Charophyta . . . . (250)   Stoneworts . . . . .MF
9. Euglenophyta . . . . (450)   Euglena . . . . F
10. Chrysophyta . . . . . . (12,502)   Diatomes, Golden-Brown
     Algae and Yellow-green
     Algae (3 classes) . . . . .MF
11. Phrrophyta . . . . (1,302)   Dinoflagellates . . . . (1,000) . . . .PM
     Pyrrophytes . . . . . (300) . . . . .PM
12. Phaeophyta . . . . (1,302)   Brown Algae, Kelp . . . . M
13. Rhodophyta . . . . (3,750)   Red Algae . . . . .MF

PLANTS	PLANTS	PLANTS	PLANTS	PLANTS	PLANTS	PLANTS

1. Bryophyta . . . . ( )   Mosses, Liverworts
     Hornworts . . . . .T
2. Tracheophyta . . . . ( )   Vascular Plants . . . . .TMF

(P=Parasitic; T=Terrestrial; M=Marine; F=Fresh Water).

ANIMALS   ANIMALS   ANIMALS   ANIMALS   ANIMALS   ANIMALS

Kingdom Animalia
Subkingdom Protozoa

PHYLA	SPECIES	NAME	HABITAT
1. Sarcomastigophora...	(18,000)	Flagellates	PTMF
2. Labyrinthulata	(38)	Protozoans	TM
3. Apicomplexa	(3,900)	Protozoans	P
4. Microspora	(1,000)	Protozoans	P
5. Myxozoa	(560)	Sporulating Organisms	P
6. Ascetospora	(21)	Sporeforming Protozoans	P
7. Ciliophora	(7,200)	Ciliates	PTMF

Subkingdom Phogocytellozoa (Placozoa)

1. Metazoa	(2)	Metazoan	P

Subkingdom Parazoa (Porifera)

1. Porifera	(5,000)	Sponges	MF

Subkingdom Eumetazoa; All other multicellular animals of 29 phyla

1. Cnidaria	(5,000)	Jellyfish, Corals, Sea Anemonies	MF
2. Ctenophora	(82)	Comb Jellyfish	M
3. Platyhelminthes	(5,500)	Flatworms, Flukes, Tapeworms	PTMF
4. Nemertea	(900)	Ribbon Worms	PTMF
5. Gnathostomulida	(83)	Jaw Worms	M
6. Mesozoa	7 genera	Ciliated organisms	PM
7. Gastrotricha	(429)	Micrometazoans	TMF
8. Rotifera	(1,500)	Rotifers	TMF
9. Loricifera	(1)	Loricifers	M
10. Kinorhyncha	(85)	Segmented Pseudocoelomates...	M
11. Nemata	(12,000)	Nematodes, Eel Worms, Roundworms	PTMF
12. Nematomorpha	(250)	Gordian or Horsehair Worms	PMF
13. Acanthocephala	(275)	Spiny—headed--worms	P
14. Priapulida	(9)	Vermiform invertebrates	M
15. Mollusca (50,000)			
CLASSES			
Caudofoveata	(70)	Vermiform	M
Solenogasters	(180)	Vermiform	M
Polyplacophora	(500)	Chitons or Coat—of—mail shells.	M
Monoplacophora	(10)	Neopilina	M
Gastropoda	(35,000)	Snails, Sea Slugs	TMF
Bivalvia	(8,000)	Clams, Mussels	MF
Scaphopoda	(350)	Tusk or Tooth Shells	M
Cephalopoda	(600)	Octopus, Squid, Cuttlefish	M

(P=Parasitic; T=Terrestrial; M=Marine; F=Fresh Water).

114

ANIMALS PHYLA	SPECIES	ANIMALS NAME	HABITAT
16. Annelida	(12,175)	Earthworms, Leeches, Polychaetes	PTMF
17. Pogonophora	(18)	Beard Worms	M
18. Echiura	(137)	Echiura	M
19. Sipuncula	(640)	Peanut Worm	M
20. Arthropoda (4 subphyla)	...	(one to 2 million species)	PTMF
Crustacea		Horseshore Crabs,	
Chelicerata		Scorpions, Spiders, Sea Spiders	
Uniramia (Myriapods and		Crabs, Shrimp, Lobster, Centipedes,	
Insects		Millipedes, Insects	
Pentastomida			
21. Onychophora	(70)	Paripatus	T
22. Tardigrada	(376)	Water Bears	MF
23. Phoronida	(10)	Phoronid	M
24. Bryozoa	(4,000)	Moss animals	M
25. Entoprocta	(150)	Entoprocts	M
26. Brachipoda	(335)	Brachiopods or Lamp Shells	M
27. Chaetognata	(70)	Arrow Worms	M
28. Echinodermata	(1,371)	Crenoids, Feather Stars and Sea Lilies	M
	(1,500)	Asteroids, Sea Stars	M
	(2,000)	Ophiuroids, Brittle Stars, Basket Stars and Snake Stars	M
	(900)	Echinoids, Sea Urchins, Sand Dollars, Heart Urchins	M
	(450)	Holothurians, Sea Cucumbers	M
29. Chordata (three subphyla)	....		
SUBPHYLA			
Cephalochordata	(23)	Amphioxus or Lancelet	M
Tunicata	(1,250)	Ascidians, Tunicates, Sea Squirts	M
Vertebrata (seven classes)	....		
Agnatha (no jaws)	(63)	Lampreys, Hagfish	MF
Chondrichthyes (jawed)	(843)	Sharks and Rays	MF
Osteichthyes (bony fish)	(18,150)	Bass, Trout, Tuna, Opah	TMF
Amphibia	(3,140)	Salamanders, Frogs, Caecilians	TF
Reptalia	(222)	Turtles	TMF
	(5,600)	Crocodilians, Lizards, Snakes, Tuatara	TMF
Aves	(9,021)	Penguins, Pelicans, Sea Gulls	TMF
Mammalia (21 orders)	(4,115)	Seals, Gray Whales, Porpoises, Sea Otter, Pilot Whales, People	TMF

(P=Parasitic; T=Terrestrial; M=Marine; F=Fresh Water).

Barbara examining a shell found at the beach. Photo by Wesley M. Farmer.

RANGE and DISTRIBUTION MAP

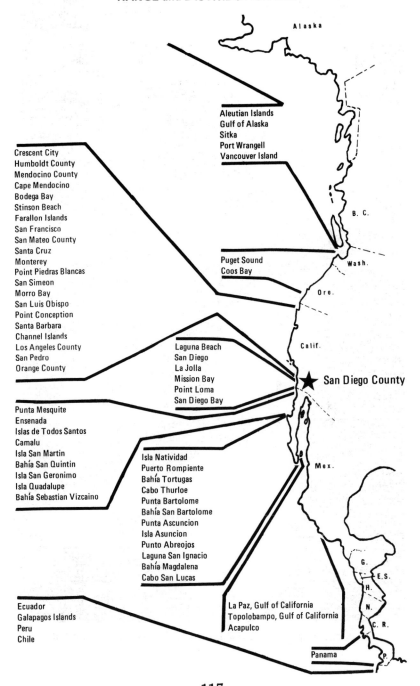

Alaska

Aleutian Islands
Gulf of Alaska
Sitka
Port Wrangell
Vancouver Island

B. C.

Crescent City
Humboldt County
Mendocino County
Cape Mendocino
Bodega Bay
Stinson Beach
Farallon Islands
San Francisco
San Mateo County
Santa Cruz
Monterey
Point Piedras Blancas
San Simeon
Morro Bay
San Luis Obispo
Point Conception
Santa Barbara
Channel Islands
Los Angeles County
San Pedro
Orange County

Puget Sound
Coos Bay

Wash.

Ore.

Calif.

Laguna Beach
San Diego
La Jolla
Mission Bay
Point Loma
San Diego Bay

★ San Diego County

Punta Mesquite
Ensenada
Islas de Todos Santos
Camalu
Isla San Martin
Bahía San Quintin
Isla San Geronimo
Isla Quadalupe
Bahía Sebastian Vizcaino

Isla Natividad
Puerto Rompiente
Bahía Tortugas
Cabo Thurloe
Punta Bartolome
Bahía San Bartolome
Punta Ascuncion
Isla Asuncion
Punto Abreojos
Laguna San Ignacio
Bahía Magdalena
Cabo San Lucas

Mex.

G.

E.S.

H.

N.

C. R.

Ecuador
Galapagos Islands
Peru
Chile

La Paz, Gulf of California
Topolobampo, Gulf of California
Acapulco

Panama

P.

INDEX

INDEX

ADDENDUM to INDEX

Discovering sealife at Casa Beach, La Jolla